HERO AND ANTI-HERO
IN THE AMERICAN FOOTBALL NOVEL

HERO AND ANTI-HERO
IN THE AMERICAN FOOTBALL NOVEL

Changing Conceptions of Masculinity
from the Nineteenth Century
to the Twenty-First Century

Donald Lee Deardorff II

The Edwin Mellen Press
Lewiston•Queenston•Lampeter

Library of Congress Cataloging-in-Publication Data

Deardorff, Donald Lee II.
    Hero and anti-hero in the American football novel : changing conceptions of
masculinity from the nineteenth century to the twenty-first century /
Donald Lee Deardorff II.
        p. cm.
    Includes bibliographical references and index.
    ISBN-13: 978-0-7734-5554-2
    ISBN-10: 0-7734-5554-X
    I. Title.

hors série.

A CIP catalog record for this book is available from the British Library.

The Edwin Mellen Press   The Edwin Mellen Press
Box 450   Box 67
Lewiston, New York   Queenston, Ontario
USA 14092-0450   CANADA L0S 1L0

The Edwin Mellen Press, Ltd.
Lampeter, Ceredigion, Wales
UNITED KINGDOM SA48 8LT

Printed in the United States of America

Table of Contents

Preface

In *Hero and Anti-Hero in the American Football Novel*, Professor Donald Deardorff addresses the well documented crisis facing men in the United States. He accurately and succinctly summarizes some of the general conclusions being drawn about men in America, sets out to name the source of the problem, and suggests a solution. His diagnosis: "at its deepest essence, masculinity is a search for meaning, a quest for a grand narrative that can be trusted" (12). He traces the quest in an analysis of masculine centers, or codes.

Masculine centers have failed men and left them bereft of a "seed for a healthy identity." Professor Deardorff traces the failure of masculine centers using the example of the football hero as a dominant contemporary masculine center. In narrative that concisely encapsulates the literature he recounts, the author makes his point that popular culture has exposed the football hero center as a deficient source for masculine identity.

The search for identity is a metaphysical search which will certainly fail if a person or society tries to satisfy the search within the physical existence. The most troubling example for me of the failed search for identity is the substitution of power for meaning. The traditional feminist critique of society places the responsibility for oppression of minorities at the feet of patriarchal male power and domination: as men exercise power and control, others invariably suffer. The present argument looks at this situation from the masculine perspective, and gives new insight into this age-old problem: "beyond power, men seek empowerment" (12). Renunciation of the pursuit for power and control is not by itself the answer to the masculine crisis because it does not fill the void men seek to fill at the outset. Men experience a "collective need ii

for redemption" (6) which will not be granted if they seek their meaning at the expense of others.

This text points its readers to an important question inherent within masculine studies: is male identity a matter of what men *do,* or who men *are*? In pointing out the manner in which males have attempted "to gain exclusive control over maleness" (28), the author places this question in a more critical light: has the search for a masculine center been misguided from the beginning—did it begin on the wrong square? This question brings the reader back to the original male dilemma of attempting to answer a metaphysical problem with a physical solution.

Professor Timothy Stanley of the University of Manchester, UK is in agreement with the thesis presented here and argues for more than a critique of the modern day man: while men are told what not to be (oppressors), they are not given another narrative to pattern themselves after. Professor Deardorff solves this dilemma by providing an alternative.

The solution lies first in what Professor Deardorff names ironic resistance. Ironic resistance is a useful first step, but he argues more is needed in order to escape the downward spiral growing from incomplete narratives that are always eventually unmasked. His suggested solution is a spirituality that encompasses both faith in the supernatural and service to others. Spirituality and service working together provide the answer to internal metaphysical needs with an external manifestation of meaning that is an alternative to raw power. This work has the potential to advance the masculine search for meaning into an area that will give more permanent results than the recycled centers that have been sampled over the centuries.

Feminist scholars have recognized that both sexes will benefit most when masculine studies are conducted alongside feminist studies. A joint attempt to theorize the intricacies of the search for meaning for men and women will increase the chances for living as equals, encouraging and sustaining one another in practical living experiences.

Adopting the theme of the book, I asked myself what would be a dominant feminist center today? Women seek meaning through choice, relationships, equality, and spirituality for example. The concept of choice in particular has grown beyond the realm of reproduction to take on iconic status for women. Feminists insist for women that they have the right to choose how to live, who to be, where to place their faith, all the while being seen as equals, respected for their contributions to society. Also, spirituality has always been important to women—women comprise today more than fifty percent of church congregations—and that is reflected within feminist scholarship. Professor Deardorff combines the feminist values of choice and spirituality when he offers a grand narrative for men that is not totalizing, recognizing that each of us has the right to choose the way we believe and how we will serve while emphasizing the essential role of faith in God or a Supreme Being. He offers a spiritual solution that is not formally religious, and, consistent with his Christianity and mine, invites others to believe, without demanding they agree with him. I, certainly along with many others, welcome him and others like him into the exercise of finding individual meaning with an internal and external focus, without insisting on a hierarchal system of preeminence. The result of such a search will bring personal peace and satisfaction, and perhaps such a blessing could benefit society at large.

Dr. Deborah B. Haffey
Professor of Communication Arts
Cedarville University
Co-Director Women of Vision

Chapter 1

Masculinity as a Search for Meaning

It seems that even under the best of circumstances masculinity has always been a problem, a package central to men's lives that is correctly labeled "handle with care." In his book, *American Manhood: Transformations in Masculinity from the Revolution to the Modern Era*, E. Anthony Rotundo recounts the story of the introduction of the term "neurasthenia" into the American medical lexicon in the year 1869. The word referred to a condition that described a large and growing number of men at the time who were suffering from stress and exhaustion. These were white, middle to upper-middle class men, married landowners who had loving wives, children, good careers, and nearly exclusive access to the avenues of power. Unlike women or minority men, they could attend college, vote, open businesses, and hold positions of power and influence; they controlled the government, education, and religious and economic institutions; they set social agendas, dictated moral codes, and even created their own myths, which, of course, lionized them. One such myth was that of the self-made man, a creature that took on many forms from 1776-1900. In post-Civil War America, the self-made man was, in Victorian middle-class terms, one who started with little, but through hard work, determination, drive, common sense, and nerve, carved himself a place in a tough man's world. Such a man was measured by his material accomplishments. He was expected to work long hours to ensure professional success; he was supposed to be a dedicated husband, a loving father, a loyal lodge member, a pious religious leader, and a sensible man of the world. Not surprisingly, fulfilling the contrary demands of this masculine identity was too much for many men. Quite simply, they broke down under the weight of an oppressive masculinity. As a group, these middle class, self-made men were among the most privileged and least challenged men in American history. Yet, they buckled under the pressure of having to live up to a dominant masculine code.[1]

The moral of the story is that masculinity, even when practiced among a group of men whose dominance in any given society seems secure, is actually volatile and as potentially harmful as it is helpful. Perhaps this is because any dominant masculine template only seems stable, its supposed position of unquestioned power being merely the stuff of illusion. In reality, the dominant code, in whatever society at whatever time in American history, has always achieved its position by suppressing many alternative codes that, though temporarily brought under its control, are always chipping away at its place atop the hierarchy of masculinities at work in the cultural matrix. As noted sociologist R. W. Connell says, "The history of masculinity ... is not linear. There is no master line of development to which all else is subordinate, no simple shift from 'traditional' to 'modern.' Rather we see ... complex structures of gender relations in which dominant, subordinated and marginalized masculinities are in constant interaction."[2] The end result of this continual flux in which masculine codes collide and challenge each other, and in which they all change in response to cultural shifts too quickly for most men to keep up, is confusion.

If white American men have struggled to achieve stability and contentment when their power remained relatively unchallenged, it's no wonder that most men feel more than a little off balance today. White men are challenged in every sector of society by men of all races, while Hispanic men have numerically drawn equal to their white counterparts in some areas of the United States. Men of all races have been forced to redefine masculine codes based on the advancement of women in business, politics, and especially in education, where girls and women have outpaced boys and men in nearly every statistical category for some time now. Gay men have forced straight men to reckon with their own sexuality. Changes in industry, communication, computer technology, and the overall economy have forced men into new work patterns, with many men being forced out of work. It is not unusual for a wife to make more money than her husband, or for a father to be the primary care-giver, establishing his domain in the domestic sphere while mom takes on the role of breadwinner, despite the fact that most of his peers will still expect him to be the parent who financially supports the family.

Such confusion is reflected in the barrage of conflicting images that rain down on men every day from televisions, radios, magazines, novels, internet sites, and an array of advertisements, drenching them in a sea of contradiction. What does it mean, for instance, to be a father? Is it to be a carefree moron, like Homer Simpson, or a loveable bumbler like Ray Romano? If you flip the channel to Nickelodeon, you might find the sobriety of Jim Douglas, the cool confidence of Mike Brady, or the paternal wisdom of Howard Cunningham to your liking. They were in their hey-day in the sixties and seventies, but they continue to exist side-by-side with their contemporary television counterparts thanks to never-ending reruns. Television is a powerful image-maker, indeed, but it is hardly the only one. Drive down the busiest strip in your town and you'll likely see uplifting billboards encouraging fathers to spend more time with their kids or men who are pictured as responsible physicians, real-estate agents, or friendly bankers, followed by angry looking men under whose picture the text reads "Stop Child Abuse" or "Report Deadbeat Dads."

The contradictions never end. Watch the evening news and you will see countless images of heroic men, soldiers fighting for the liberation of oppressed peoples, policemen serving the public, or public servants trying to correct societal problems, whom any boy would be proud to call dad; however, you will also see that most of the oppression, crime, and social problems are being caused or exacerbated by men acting as terrorists, criminals, or social deviants. No venue is without conflict. Consider athletics, long a hallowed arena for many men. Sports fans are used to heroic field generals and courageous veterans whose tremendous athletic feats on the field are rivaled by their commitment to community service, but they are equally accustomed to spoiled millionaires whose sexual irresponsibility is matched only by a level of immaturity and greed that is hardly paternal.

Of course, the confusion is hardly limited to men who are fathers. Boys and men of all ages are surrounded by a wild array of conflicting myths that swirl around them in diverse cultural packaging. Should one be a warrior who is defined by his capacity for violence, as suggested by Bruce Lee, Steven Segal, or Jean-Claude Van Damme films? Or, should one aspire to define oneself around a model of sensitivity and caring, as suggested by the men in *Madame Butterfly* or *Angels in America*? Both are problematic. Displays of force may make one feel manly, but in the long run violence usually results in the destruction of its perpetrators. Sensitivity and gentleness simply don't play well in many venues, where toughness and competitiveness are so highly valued. The star athlete is another tempting template, but it has its problems. Only a few can attain such lofty status, and those who do often have to sacrifice their bodies, education, or emotional development. Plus, like so many templates for the young, the athlete and his glory fade quickly. Closely related to the athlete is the image of the all-American boy, the kid who excels at sports, is a good scholar, has many friends including a beautiful girlfriend, wins the respect of both his peers and adults, is psychologically balanced, defends the weak, and dispenses justice with fairness and equanimity. Even though it is an identity that is impossible to maintain, the myth of the well-rounded young man still survives, even as it is upended and made fun of at every turn. Within the boundaries of the same school or town, the all-American boy can be both admired and despised, with many boys winding up dazed and confused within a whirlwind of conflicting stories.

Of course, there are many other roles and accompanying myths that tempt boys and men. The soldier has often held an honored, romantic place in the minds of young men, but the soldier leads a hard life with low pay, spends long periods away from loved ones, and sometimes dies for causes he may or may not believe in. The "ladies' man," the stud for lack of a better term, has always been admired in male circles; however, sexual conquest is at best on the outs and the ladies' man is seen as a bit of joke; at worst, macho behavior is simply a form of sexual harassment. For years, if you didn't want to be a hero of some type, you could be a rebel. Even into the fifties and sixties, films such as *Rebel Without a Cause* and *The Wild One* celebrated the power of the anti-hero. But where is the power of the rebel today? It seems non-existent. Whether one fashions oneself as an artist, hippie, skater, motorhead, racer, dropout, hipster, goth, gangster, or moop, it will likely seem forced and artificial. Even the coolness of the rebel is now uncool. The quality PBS film, *Merchants of Cool*, is a wonderful resource for understanding how the American industry, especially the media, thrive off identity confusion. For nearly every identity one can have as a young man has been conceived, co-opted, promoted, and just as quickly ridiculed by media forces that both package and sell coolness to young men even as they undermine that very coolness. In the process, two things have been exposed. The first is that none of these templates of cool are actually achievable; the second is that even if they were, they would not satisfy the needs of any young man.[3] In summary, the contradiction is as follows: hundreds of images say: be the breadwinner, be the conqueror, be the aggressor, be the sexual hero, be the athlete, the soldier, the husband, the rebel, the artist, the hippie, etc., and yet, don't be any of those things because they are harmful, silly, a joke. Where do you go when all of the myths still circulate even as they are continuously exposed? It's disorienting. As scholar Gene Veith, Jr. says of postmodern culture, "If there are no absolutes, if truth is relative, then there can be no stability, no meaning in life. If reality is socially constructed, then moral guidelines are only masks for oppressive power and individual liberty is an illusion."[4]

The confusion is further evidenced in the way academics have addressed masculinity. Any perusal of titles in an academic library will reveal the angst that surrounds masculinity. Consider Warren Rosenberg's *Legacy of Rage*, James McBride's *War, Battering, And Other Sports: The Gulf Between American Men and Women,* Stephen Boyd's *Redeeming Men: Religion and Masculinities,* Stephen Norwood's *Strikebreaking & Intimidation: Mercenaries and Masculinity in*

Twentieth-Century America, Michael Schwalbe's *Unlocking the Iron Cage: The Men's Movement, Gender Politics, and American Culture,* Russell West's *Subverting Masculinity: Hegemonic and Alternative Versions of Masculinity in Contemporary Culture,* Marilyn Wesley's *Violent Adventure: Contemporary Fiction of American Men,* Warren Steinberg's *Masculinity: Identity, Conflict, and Transformation,* Renford Reese's *American Paradox: Young Black Men,* T. Walter Herbert's *Sexual Violence and American Manhood,* or Greg Forter's *Murdering Masculinities: Fantasies of Gender and Violence in the American Crime Novel.* The titles, just like the pages of the books themselves, drip with the anger, pain and torment that, in the view of many academics, characterizes masculinity, a trait that seemingly is chiefly defined by its need to be overcome, to be redeemed. Men's collective need for redemption is underscored by nearly every serious work on manhood and masculinity. *Masculinity, Bodies, Movies, Culture*, edited by Peter Lehman, is a good example. Some of the articles include, Krin Gabbard's "'Someone is Going to Pay': Resurgent White Masculinity in *Ransom,*" Lehman's "Crying Over the Melodramatic Penis: Melodrama and Male Identity in Films of the 90s," Joe Wlodarz's "Rape Fantasies: Hollywood and Homophobia," Robert Lang and Maher Ben Moussa's "Choosing to Be 'Not a Man': Masculine Anxiety in Nouri Bouzid's *Rih Essed/Man of Ashes,*" Susan White's "T(he)-Men's Room: Masculinity and Space in Anthony Mann's *T-Men,*" Dennis Bingham's "Oliver Stone's *Nixon* and the Unmanning of the Self-Made Man," and last, but surely not least, Sally Robinson's "'Emotional Constipation' and the Power of Damned Masculinity: *Deliverance*: and the Paradoxes of Male Liberation." Constipation indeed.

Is there a way to make sense of the confusing world of masculinity and the horrible tensions that so many men feel? Most scholars are unified in answering in the affirmative, and they are nearly as unified regarding their explanation of the problem. In fact, the crux of the dilemma, in the eyes of most scholars, can be summed up in one word: power. The theory goes something like this. Men have always primarily defined themselves in terms of power; they have sought it over a number of "others," and they have feared humiliation at the hands of those who have power. Masculinity is most clearly viewed as either one or the other of these things. A man is either concerned for how he can control others or he is seeking to avoid emasculation by a more powerful person or institution. Masculinity, then, can be looked at as a test that never ends; for a man must continually engage a paradigm of conflict that will leave him feeling either superior or "unmanned." The world is made up of adversaries, "others," and a man is measured by his ability to control them.

By far, most contemporary scholars have focused on men's fear of women, generally concluding that traditionally masculinity has been derived from men either controlling women or, at the very least, avoiding all behaviors that might be considered feminine; for such behavior might earn one the nickname "Mary" or "sissy," and thus the humiliation a man seeks to avoid. A good example of feminist scholarship is *Masculinity Studies & Feminist Theories: New Directions*, edited by Judith Kegan Gardiner. Every essay in the book explains a different facet of the patriarchy, that overarching monolith whose name signifies the oppression of women by men everywhere. For instance, in "The Enemy Outside: Thoughts on the Psychodynamics of Extreme Violence with Special Attention to Men and Masculinity," Nancy Chodorow says that masculinity is so inextricably tied to the conquest of women by men in nearly every way possible that the only healthy alternative for both sexes is to obliterate the concept of masculinity as we know it. According to Chodorow, the same is true of femininity, which is nothing more than men's conception of what women should be. Both masculinity and femininity must be blurred until there is a "dislodging of the phallus."[5]

The fear of just such a dislodging has been the subject of many literary, art history, and cinematic studies. For instance, in *Murdering Masculinities*, Greg Forter examines the evolution of the crime novel from Dashiell Hammett to Chester Himes, concluding that the genre is primarily characterized by "its preoccupation with violence. And that violence typically includes a misogyny by which the male hero defines himself by vanquishing a feminine principle that threatens his 'sense of a discrete self.'"[6] The male reader aligns himself with the hard-boiled hero as he vanquishes all things feminine. Donna Campbell insists that the same fear of effeminacy characterizes the novels of many male writers from 1885-1915. She focuses on the works of Harold Frederick and Frank Norris, contending that *The Damnation of Theron Ware* and *Vandover and the Brute* display the fear that men felt around the turn of the century as women began to make some inroads on previously all-male bastions. Both novels emphasize the moral laxity believed to come with feminization, a quality that weakens a man, making him ripe for the type of downfall suffered by the male protagonists of both novels.[7] Power has also been a central motif for male artists. Barbara Melosh's *Gender and American History Since 1890* is one of several fine works that uses art to track the history of gender in the United States. In one essay entitled "Manly Work," Melosh explains that the reason for a turn to highly masculinized art featuring portraits of working class men between 1935 and 1950 was the fact that patriarchal power was being threatened by a number of sources, including women's political and economic gains in the face of men's losses caused by the depression and World War II. According to Melosh, "the figure of the manly worker embodied nostalgia for an imagined past of individual dignity lost in the modern world of work." For every *Rosie the Riveter* there were hundreds of paintings of construction workers, metal workers, and laborers: "The manly worker of public art bracketed the shame of unemployment by putting it out of sight, replacing it with the ideal of labor."[8] Of course, many of these themes have been echoed in cinematic studies, such as *Me Jane: Masculinity, Movies and Women*, edited by Pat Kirkham and Janet Thumin. The editors affirm that "power and masculinity are virtually synonymous," and because masculinity "is in need of constant reinforcement," it calls for men to continually keep women under their control. Indeed, all of the essays in the book drive home this point: From Jimmy Cagney slapping a grapefruit into his girlfriend's face in *Public Enemy* (1934) to Richard Gere rescuing a prostitute from a life of degradation in *Pretty Woman* (1987), masculinity on the silver screen often involves some type of conquest of female interests.[9]

Women, however, are not the only objects of conquest by men whose identities are formed primarily by power. Other men are quite often targets. Whether at war, on a sports field, in the boardroom, or in any other area where men are pitted against each other, the goal is to make oneself a winner at the expense of the other guy; to humiliate him. Mark Hussey's *Masculinities: Interdisciplinary Readings* contains an essay by Paul Kivel entitled "The 'Act Like a Man Box'"in which the author contends that masculinity puts men in a power box in which all of their relationships with other men are defined by their ability to best them in some way, shape, or form. The result is usually fear, isolation, anger, or rejection.[10] An even more disturbing book is James McBride's *War, Battering, and Other Sports*, in which he argues that masculinity can be understood by examining the relationship between war, sports like football, and domestic violence. Men have always waged war to solve problems and they have always relied on the threat of physical violence to dominate the domestic sphere. Even their games celebrate the acquisition of territory through brutalizing one's opponent.[11] McBride's book may be a bit extreme, but he is only slightly more outspoken than many other authors on masculinity, most of whom see men stagnating in an ongoing zero sum game of dominance and humiliation.

Especially at risk in this power game are minority men and gay men. Already in a vulnerable position, black men have been easy targets for their white counterparts for most of American history. Renford Reese explains the situation nicely in his book, *American Paradox: Young Black Men*. Masculinity has always been defined by power and black men have always been denied access to the avenues of power. If you can't go to school, vote, hold a well-paying job, run for office, or run a business, you don't have much of a chance to compete against other men. In fact, you become the fodder on which the men with power, in this case, middle to upper class white men, cut their teeth. This legacy of humiliation and disempowerment is so deeply ingrained in black culture that Reese feels young black men continue to feel its effects today.[12] Of course, this experience is not limited to black men. Warren Rosenberg's *Legacy of Rage: Jewish Masculinity, Violence, and Culture* relates a short history of Jewish men in the United States, a history in which Jews have been forced to adopt violent postures because they were denied access to traditional roads to power. Several of the essays in Franklin Ng's *Asian Americans: Reconceptualizing Culture, History, Politics* tell a similar tale for Asian-American men, who have found themselves at the mercy of dominant, white masculine codes by which white men have not only devalued Asian masculinities, but have also deliberately sought to make themselves feel powerful at the expense of Asian-Americans. Perhaps no group of men has been as feared and misunderstood as gay men. Above all other men, it seems that straight men of all races have sought to distance themselves from the specter of homosexuality. As Suzanne Phurr points out in her essay, "Homophobia as a Weapon of Sexism," located in Paula Rothenberg's *Race, Class and Gender in the United States: An Integrated Study*, to avoid being called gay or prissy has been to avoid humiliation; to be manly is to demonstrate one's power over gay men and straight men who are branded as feminine.[13] For those interested in art history, Sarah Burns' *Inventing the Modern Artist: Art and Culture in Gilded Age America* provides an illuminating examination of how at the turn of the century straight artists painted highly traditional, masculine self-portraits as a defense against the aesthetic and decadent movements in art. So afraid were they of Oscar Wilde and his cronies, that many artists put a great deal of work into satirizing them, showing their alleged moral weaknesses, and making every attempt to disassociate homosexuality from art or the artist.[14]

Other scholars have written about men displaying their masculinity by maintaining power over technology, laws, language, or knowledge, but the story essentially remains a one-dimensional tale of men defining themselves by acquiring power and denying it to others by using whatever means are considered valuable by their society. Over the last half-century, however, this has gotten much harder for men to do. As mentioned earlier, the country has changed a great deal since World

War II. I wonder how many white men, or most men for that matter, of my generation thought we would see women routinely outnumbering men in medical schools, law schools, and MBA programs? How many would have thought of themselves living as a minority in a predominantly Hispanic neighborhood? How many were prepared for a corporate jungle where they would be a faceless number trying to survive in an environment where the laws no longer seem to favor them, and sometimes seem to work against them? How many thought that *Will and Grace,* one of the first television shows to treat homosexuality as completely normal and male heterosexuals as, well, problematic at best, would be a top ten program for several years running? Probably not very many; perhaps the same number that would have thought they would have to feel guilty about having power or material wealth, or about being a man at all. This condition of confusion, of great expectations met by a changing and sometimes bewildering present time, has not been lost on scholars. Most agree that many American men are confused and that they feel threatened on any number of fronts: politically, economically, socially, religiously, domestically, and even athletically, where it has become clear that even that longtime male bastion of sports, perhaps the last holdout of men who wanted to define themselves against woman as other, is as much a female domain as it is a preserve for patriarchal, masculine norms. The bottom line for most scholars is that however you slice it, men expected power and they are not going to get it on the old terms. This has given rise to a kind of panic, a sense of not knowing what to do or how to define oneself.[15]

I do not intend to dispute that this theory of masculinity as power and its corresponding conclusions about the current "crisis in masculinity" is not partially correct. There is far too much evidence in its favor for me to do that. However, I am contending that the power theory is only partially accurate. It has its flaws. For instance, one problem that most scholars have not addressed is the question of why, throughout American history, most privileged men who have enjoyed incredible power have not felt terribly secure about their masculinity. What about all those men who reaped the benefits and rewards of power, but who were never happy? Think about all those men suffering from nurasthenia, or of the countless men driven to acquire more and more power and possessions, but who were never satisfied by the endeavors. Scholars might argue that this is simply the nature of patriarchy, that in and of itself it is a trap that sucks one into a vortex of unquenchable desire for power and conquest that can never truly produce contentment. I would not disagree, but I would hasten to ask exactly why it never brings happiness,, and if it cannot bring happiness, what should men do instead to fashion an identity? On these questions, scholars have produced answers which, from my point of view, are unsatisfactory. Feminists have suggested gender equity; Marxists have called for class equality; environmentalists want a respect for and a reconnection with nature; psychologists and psychiatrists have alerted us to the importance of maintaining our intricate inner wiring; postcolonial theorists have recommended recognizing the dangers of the colonialist impulse and embracing the other; new age gurus want us to get in touch with our inner child; many religions say to connect with God or supernatural energy in the universe; some postmodernists recommend a type of humanistic hedonism, doing whatever you like to please yourself as long as you don't hurt anyone. Most of these folks are sincere, and many have good points. After all, most of us like the idea of boys and girls being treated equally, of protecting our environment, or of improving the lot of poor people. Still, these solutions have not satisfied men. That is because they do not address the deeper problem that surrounds masculinity. For the truth is that masculinity is only partly a quest for power. I would even go as far as to say that the quest for power and avoidance of humiliation is a bastardized perversion of true masculinity. At is deepest essence, masculinity is a search for meaning, a quest for a grand narrative that can be trusted. Beyond power, men seek empowerment. They want to be able to act in the context of a master story that can be trusted. This is my theory about how to best understand masculinity and its evolution in the United States. When scholars begin to address the deeper nature of masculinity, they will likely offer more satisfying solutions.

Perhaps the most powerful testament to the fact that men's ultimate quest has been for meaning over material comfort can be found in the field of religion. From the anthropomorphic gods of Greece and Rome to the big three religions, Christianity, Judaism, and Islam, to many other religious creeds, men in the West have relied on their faith to sustain them. In addition, one can mine the fields of anthropology, philosophy, sociology, psychology, history, and the sciences for evidence that desire for meaning has been and continues to be a potent driving force for men. Of course, there is abundant literary evidence that men have always desired meaning more than power, and this is my primary interest.

Most of the great books of the Western world, it seems, are about a male protagonist who is seeking to make sense of a confusing world by finding and following some code which he believes is anchored in truth. Homer's *Iliad* tells the tale of Achilles, who seeks honor and fame by following the Greek code of the whole man, balancing physical, mental and spiritual values while defending the state. *The Aeneid* reflects the Roman version of the state hero made in the ideal of the myths of the Republic. The Old English period gives us the epic *Beowulf*, whose hero embodies the old Germanic heroic code of boasting, mighty physical feats, and generosity to one's retainers. At the end of the Middle Ages is Thomas Malory's *Morte d'Arthur*, an early tribute to chivalry with Arthur, Lancelot, and the other knights of the roundtable performing noble deeds, while earning the love of virtuous women. The Renaissance is defined by works such as Castiglione's *The Courtier*, in which the hero learns to live out a perfectionist's humanist code; the reader is instructed on the importance not only of physical exploits such as riding and fencing, but learns such things as the art of elocution and the writing of love poetry. Much more specialized is Machiavelli's *The Prince*, which is essentially a guide for young lords and princes that instructs them that when it comes to power the ends justify the means and that the measure of a ruler is his ability to adapt so that he can maintain control under changing circumstances. Shakespeare's greatest men earn their merits by following a noble narrative that they believe to be true, and his tragedies are dominated by heroes who are consistently tormented because they cannot adopt a code by which to act. As Hamlet says, "To be or not to be, that is the question," a statement which reveals the young Dane's deep desire to find a rationale by which to act. Still, the Renaissance is also defined by Christian works such as John Bunyan's *The Pilgrim's Progress,* Dante's *The Divine Comedy*, and Milton's *Paradise Lost*, where the heroes are saved and the outcasts damned by how they measure up to a Christian code based on the sacred scripture of the *Bible*. Christian themes continued to be prominent in the 19th century in works such as Goethe's *Faust*, but would be rivaled in that century by several movements, including the romanticism of Wordsworth, Coleridge, Shelley, Byron, and Keats, which advocated a manhood based on a spiritual connection with nature and a spirit of sublimity that runs through the universe; the Victorian middle-class propriety evidenced in the novels of Dickens, Collins, and Thackery; and the wild aestheticism of Wilde, Gide, Zola, and Huymans, whose code of sensual indulgence would presage the permissiveness of the nineteen twenties, sixties, and seventies. The twentieth century would see all of the above codes rehashed in new forms and the ascendancy of others as well, including lost generation nihilism, the shallow, image-driven materialism that has been so dominant since the end of World War II, and postmodern pastiche.

Certainly, this longing for meaning characterizes the best of American literature. Consider Melville's *Moby Dick*, which is narrated by Ishmael, who relates the story of Ahab, a man who pursues the great white whale that comes to symbolize the great and elusive meaning of the universe. It is understanding that Ahab desires and the character that both he and Ishmael admire most in the novel is Queequeg, the savage tribesman who has complete faith in his little statue, Yojo. The western reader is tempted to think of Queequeg as simple and foolish to believe in the goodness of such an idol, but he is happy, content, and fulfilled, everything that Ishmael in particular so steadfastly desires. As Charles Haberstroh comments, "Queequeg is so attractive to Ishmael because he is ... a figure of enormous psychological stability compared to Ishmael. He does not go through the discursive mental gymnastics Ishmael does, because he already possesses the integration of personality that Ishmael can only hope for."[16] The desperate need for significance and understanding in *Moby Dick* is similar to that seen in the works of another great nineteenth century novelist, Mark Twain, whose *Mysterious Stranger* features a narrator on a quest to understand how the world works and what his function should be. Twain explores whether or not God exists, if there are supernatural forces of good and evil controlling us, how much free will we have as we try to control our fate, and whether or not we can ever hope to circumvent fate. The quest for meaning remains the central theme of the best 19th century American literature, including such novels as William Dean Howell's *The Rise of Silas Lapham*, Rebecca Harding Davis' *Life in the Iron Mills*, Henry James' *The American*, Stephen Crane's *The Red Badge of Courage*, Frank Norris' *Mcteague*, Theodore Dreiser's *The Financier*, and a host of others.

The desire for meaning is even more pervasive in twentieth-century American literature. Earnest Hemingway's *The Sun Also Rises* reflects an entire generation's questions about the stability of religion, science and tradition. The author advances his famous code of grace under pressure as the true measure of a man who must display courage and search for meaning even as he believes that the search will prove to be fruitless. John Steinbeck's *The Grapes of Wrath* reveals an author who wants to redefine Christianity in more humanistic terms so that the human race can forge a new grand narrative on which to rely. Ralph Ellison's *Invisible Man* tells the story of a black man whose deepest lament is not being black in white America, but rather being existentially invisible; he longs for a master narrative that will grant him visibility and significance more than he does racial equality. Written around the same time, Sloan Wilson's *Man in the Gray Flannel Suit* chronicles the disintegration of a man who follows his culture's philosophical recipe for success; Wilson exposes the hollowness of the American Dream, which clearly lacks a spiritual dimension. Chaim Potok's *My Name is Asher Lev* tells the story of a young man who tries to sort through religious and parental pressures to define himself as an artist. Much like *The Chosen* and *The Promise*, the novel is an autobiographical tale of a young man trying to find out what the point of life is. Leslie Marmon Silko's *Ceremony* is similar. It is the story of Tayo, a young Laguna man trying to reconnect with a powerful story that can sustain him in the face of life's difficulties. He has been taught white ways, but is sick and near death until he begins to relearn the religious stories of the Laguna tribe. His belief in the Laguna master story saves his life. In *End Zone*, Don DeLillo assembles a group of football players at small Logos College in West Texas where they search for, what else, the Word. When they don't find meaning, they fall apart; money, sensual delight, and conquest is not enough to sustain them. Philip Roth's *My Life as a Man* has as its subject a man who sees through many of the things in which his society invests importance; he grows tremendously throughout the novel, but eventually fails because, while he can see the flaws in false centers, he can never find a reliable center of meaning on which to base his life. Similar is John Updike's *Rabbit* novels, in which Rabbit Angstrom tries nearly every culturally sanctioned template of manhood imaginable; he rejects them all in time and ultimately remains unfulfilled because he cannot find a master narrative that he believes to be true. Most recently, Tony Kushner's *Angels in America* makes one recall Twain's themes in *Mysterious Stranger*: Where is God? Who are we? Why are we here? What should we be doing? These are the questions which still dominate men's lives.

Certainly, men have always tried to answer these questions, and even a brief survey of American culture reveals that they have advanced many masculine centers, hoping that they might act as stable narratives, the stability resulting from the center being rooted in a reliable grand narrative. It seems as though most of these centers can be grouped into five dominant categories: the rugged individualist, the man of conquest, the hero, the American dreamer, and the religious man.

Over the centuries, American rugged individualism has taken many forms, but all of them have centered around men making meaning of their lives by physically mastering their environment. Perhaps the quintessential example of this center is Natty Bumppo of James Fennimore Cooper's *Leatherstocking Tales*. Muscular, level-headed, clever, and experienced, Bumppo tamed the wilderness just as Americans themselves were heading to the frontier. The wild, burly woodsman felled trees, braved harsh weather conditions, fought wild animals, strong-armed mountain ruffians, and dealt firmly and justly with Indians. A few decades later, Daniel Boone and Davy Crockett, two actual frontiersmen handy with guns, knives, and fists, would supplant Bummpo in the pages of paperback novels as the hero of young boys all over the United States in 19th century, with Boone appealing mostly to rising middle class, Victorian sensibilities and Crockett moving in for Bummpo as the hero of the common man.[17] Even when the frontier began to vanish for good at the end of the century, rugged individualism continued to manifest itself in various occupations including the firefighter, the butcher, the blacksmith, the farmer, the cowboy, and eventually the hard-boiled private detective made famous in the mid-twentieth century novels of Dashiel Hammett. Rugged individualism has become harder to achieve in the current corporate age with its emphasis on technology and teamwork, but it still permeates our culture, as evidenced by the proliferation of such films as *Unforgiven*, *Braveheart*, or *Alexander*, all of which celebrate the self-sufficient man of our mythic past.

Closely related to the rugged individualist is the man of conquest who, operating within a paradigm of conflict, achieves meaning by consistently defeating some "other." The soldier has always been the epitome of man of conquest. Though often operating in group context, he nonetheless makes meaning of his world by vanquishing the enemy. For most of his history, the soldier has enjoyed a highly romanticized reputation, which has lasted even into the modern age. As former soldier Ron Kovic writes in *Born on the Fourth of July*, "John Wayne in *The Sands of Iwo Jima* became one of my heroes. On Saturdays after the movies, ... we turned the woods into a battlefield. We set ambushes, then led gallant attacks. Then we would walk out of the woods like the heroes we knew we would become when we were men."[18] Kovic's novel is one of many that exposes the dangers of the masculinity of conquest, dangers which are even more apparent in this template's other variations. For example, there is the ever-snarling bully, who generates meaning through the humiliation of others. There are far too many of these men about; they are often our criminals and they are far too often cultivated on our city streets and schoolyards. Consider poet Jonathan Holden's description of the bully as a B-52 bomber armed to kill: "The B-52 would give you the finger from hot cars. It laid rubber, it spit, it went around in gangs, it got its finger wet and sneered about it. It beat the shit out of fairies."[19] Holden knew that America's mentality of conquest is sewed into its young men early in their lives; it is the mentality of the bully and the bully nation, one that seeks to solve problems by imposing its will on others. Perhaps a less obvious manifestation of this masculine template is the corporate warrior, as seen in novels such as Tom Wolfe's *Bonfire of the Vanities*, Bret Easton Ellis' *American Psycho*, or Jane Smiley's *Good Faith*, the man who leads his company in its quest to squash all competition even as he himself is taking down all opponents on his way to the top.

Some might argue that the most powerful and pervasive masculine template is that of the hero, defined here as the ultimate community man; there can be almost as many types of heroes as there are communities, even subcultures, to sanction their heroism. In the United States, we have seen the rise and fall of war heroes, statesmen, reformers, activists, clergymen, fathers, artists, actors, musicians, writers, athletes, and even rebels, who have served as icons of manhood for various groups of men. These men inspire other men because they represent the ultimate in the eyes of the people who look up to them; like all role models, they are paragons of meaning. Consider the popularity of Jack Kerouac's *On the Road*, whose anti-hero Sal Paradise hits the road in search of meaning beyond the conventions of middle-class America. Sal and his sidekick Dean remain heroes to countless young men to this day. By contrast, another of the most compelling centers for young men has been the ever-present but ever-changing template of the all-American boy, a curious amalgam of many of the above heroic models whose mixture has varied depending on historical circumstances. Most recently, an all-American boy might be a combination of a scholar and an athlete with a bent toward religion and a reputation for impeccable character. That he might have some artistic talent and a pretty girlfriend wouldn't hurt his cause either. Of course, like all heroic templates, the all-American boy has as many variations as there are communities in the United States.

A more distinctly American center of meaning is that of the American dreamer, a man who lives out the dominant paradigm of success of his time. For much of the country's history that has been a combination of professional, consumerist, and domestic achievement. In the late nineteenth century, for instance, many Americans admired the common man who, like the fictional Horatio Alger, rose from rags to riches via hard work and the strength of his moral character. If one didn't always acquire wealth, he might at least gain a high degree of comfort and status. In the twentieth century, the template would take on a more middle-class feel, the idea being to work hard so that you might get a good job; marry an attractive, loyal wife; have well-behaved, talented children; and be able to afford a house, a car (then two cars), a television, and a slew of other reasonably affordable possessions which would contribute to one's ability to enjoy life and to claim oneself a success. Thus, a man might become a dependable breadwinner, a loving husband and father, and a professional success. There are also novels such as *Peyton Place* and *The Man in the Gray Flannel Suit* which reflect the limitations of this center, and with the breakdown of the family in the late twentieth century, the American dream seems to have morphed into a horrible blend of comfort, images, and distraction, often via such things as jet skiing, bungee jumping, violent video games, and spectator sports with their accompanying fantasy leagues. The breadwinning father is still there, but he seems to be overshadowed by the less family-oriented man whose desire for sensual pleasure and pleasant distraction overrides the more noble domestic and professional goals of his 1950s counterpart.

Finally, there is religion, the most ancient and international of all centers of meaning that American men have adopted in a wide variety of forms. For much of the nation's history, Christianity has been the favored faith of American men, as reflected in such classic novels as Nathaniel Hawthorne's *The Scarlet Letter*, Harriet Beacher Stowe's *Uncle Tom's Cabin*, or Harold Frederick's *The Damnation of*

Theron Ware, all of which celebrated both the pleasure and pain associated with religious belief. Certainly, Christian practice has been reinvented in many forms in the twentieth century. One of the more interesting turn of events has been the sudden rise of the Promise Keepers movement in the late nineties, which was itself an outgrowth of a powerful Evangelical movement in the United States. The last century also saw powerful novels like Chaim Potok's *The Chosen* and Philip Roth's *The Ghost Writer*, which celebrated the experience of young men growing up in the Jewish tradition at mid-century. Countless books appear in university libraries and even on the shelves of local bookstores about men and Buddism, Hinduism, Islam, and many other religions; all of these books attempt to tell men how to use the dictates of the faith to find meaning and therefore peace in their lives. Recently, the rise in popularity of new-age religions and the mythopoetic men's movement reveals that, though its face may change, religion continues to be a powerful center for male identity.

While it is useful to categorize masculine types, it is more important to ask oneself several questions about all of this. How do these centers gain ascendancy in any given society at any given time? Why don't they last? Why do they later reappear in altered forms, especially since they were dismissed as being unsatisfactory in the past? Then, there is also the issue of just what it is, if anything, that ties these templates together. Is there a process at work here by which we can understand how masculinity, no matter what template or type we are talking about, works?

To answer these questions, I put one masculine center under the microscope. I examined the template of the football hero, a variant of the athletic hero that has been so influential over the course of the twentieth century. What I found is that the football hero is similar to every other masculine template in that it is characterized by the same process of masculinity; the process can be described as follows. First, inspired by cultural conditions that give rise to new realities, and especially new fears, men reinvent age-old masculine centers (ie: the hero) that allow them to create what seem to be solid, gratifying identities that appear to be permanent, natural and trustworthy. One of the most important things to remember is that any given center, in addition to appearing stable and reliable, is attractive at its height because it allows men to address the most powerful circumstances of their day.

Second, once the template has reached its height of power, it begins to suffer from exposure. It is revealed to be at best partially true and at worst emotionally or physically dangerous, and it is thus roundly criticized. In the long run, it will often be rejected by many of its former adherents. For these thoughtful men, the template usually recedes to the margins of their lives. In addition, as the cultural conditions that gave rise to the center's effectiveness fade into the sunset, the center fades as well. The big thing to remember, however, is that in the eyes of most men there is no ultimate center, one that could be considered to be rooted in what some call absolute truth, waiting to replace the departing template. Thus, only one thing can happen. Men will adopt another culturally inspired, man-made model which in time will prove to be yet another "false center" in the sense that it purports to be rooted in a stable discourse, but is in reality flawed. Eventually, the discarded center will make its way back into the limelight in a slightly different form that is more in line with the psychological needs of the men of the day. This reinvention and return to prominence is the third step in the life of a masculine template.

This process gives rise to an odd condition. The thinking man knows that any masculine center, no matter how solid it seems at any given time in history, is man-made, volatile, relatively inaccessible except to a few who can actually live it out, and otherwise full of hidden pitfalls. Any such center that a man consciously or unconsciously adopts will have to be rejected, but in favor of what? Since there seems to be no ultimate center, in the words of French philosopher Jacques Derrida no "transcendent signified," how can men ever construct and embrace a masculine center rooted in stable ground? There seems to be nowhere to turn except to another false center. Clearly, men must simultaneously embrace and reject these centers. The seemingly contradictory acceptance and rejection is what I call *ironic resistance*, the fundamental characteristic of American masculinity.

Thus, the question becomes, how do we negotiate ironic resistance? I will attempt to answer that question in this book as I discuss the origins and evolution of the football hero in a way that will hopefully allow us to understand the process of masculinity, the confusion that usually results from that process, and some ways of coping with that process. Some might wonder why, of all the masculine centers I could have chosen to illustrate my points, I chose the football hero. According to my theory, I could have chosen any template since they all reveal the same process at work, but I chose the football hero because I feel that it is representative of the possibilities and pitfalls for men in the early twenty-first century. Sport is one of the arenas with which men most want to identify themselves, and football is perhaps the most popular sport for boys and men in America, one that cuts across all races, classes, and ages. In addition, when one looks at sports literature over the course of the twentieth century, one can see that the football hero occupies a great deal of privileged space, so much so that it is hard to deny the appeal that the football hero has had for men and boys over the years. Finally, the combination of extreme adoration and criticism of the football hero proved to be irresistible. For though he is loved, he is also disliked, and this concurrent embrace and rejection is the heart of ironic resistance.

Notes

[1] E. Anthony Rotundo, *American Manhood: Transformations from the Revolution to the Modern Era* (New York: Basic Books, 1993) 186.

[2] Robert W. Connell, "The History of Masculinity," *The Masculinity Studies Reader* eds. Rachel Adams and David Savran (Malden, MA: Blackwell, 2002) 254.

[3] Barak Goldman, *Merchants of Cool* (Boston: WGBH Educational Foundation, 2001).

[4] Gene E. Veith, *Postmodern Times: A Christian Guide to Contemporary Theory and Culture* (Wheaton, IL: Crossway Books, 1994) 72.

[5] Nancy Chodorow, "The Enemy Outside: Thoughts on the Psychodynamics of Extreme Violence with Special Attention to Men and Masculinity," *Masculinity Studies & Feminist Theories: New Directions* ed. Judith Kegan Gardiner (New York: Columbia University Press, 2002) 257.

[6] Greg Forter, *Murdering Masculinities: Fantasies of Gender and Violence in the American Crime Novel* (New York: New York University Press, 2000) 25.

[7] Donna Campbell, *Resisting Regionalism: Gender and Naturalism in American Fiction: 1885-1915* (Athens, OH: Ohio University Press, 1997) 75-108.

[8] Barbara Melosh, ed., *Gender and American History Since 1890* (New York: Routledge, 1993) 177.

[9] Pat Kirkham and Janet Thumin, eds, *Me Jane: Masculinity, Movies and Women* (New York: St. Martin's, 1995) 16-18.

[10] Paul Kivel, "The 'Act Like a Man' Box," *Masculinities: Interdisciplinary Readings* ed. Mark Hussey (Upper Saddle River, NJ: Prentice-Hall, 2003) 69-71.

[11] James McBride, *War, Battering and Other Sports* (Atlantic Highlands, NJ: Humanities Press, 1995) 8-11.

[12] Renford Reese, *American Paradox: Young Black Men* (Durham, NC: Carolina Academic Press, 2004) 61-102.

[13] Suzanne Phurr, "Homophobia as a Weapon of Sexism," *Race, Class and Gender in the United States: An Integrated Study* ed. Paula Rothenberg (New York: St. Martin's Press, 1992) 431-441.

[14] Sarah Burns, *Inventing the Modern Artist* (New Haven: Yale University Press, 1996) 79-120.

[15] Ronald F. Levant, "The Masculinity Crisis," *The Men's Studies Journal* 5 (February, 1997) 221-231.

[16] Charles J. Haberstroh, *Melville and Male Identity* (Rutherford, NJ: Farleigh Dickinson University Press, 1980) 95.

24

[17] David M. Lubin, *Picturing a Nation: Art and Social Change in Nineteenth Century America* (New Haven: Yale University Press, 1994) 55-107.

[18] Ron Kovic, *Born on the Fourth of July* (New York: McGraw-Hill, 1976) 55.

[19] Jonathon Holden, "Why We Bombed Haiphong," *Real Things: An Anthology of Popular Culture in American Poetry* eds. Jim Ellidge and Susan Swartwont (Bloomington, IN: Indiana University Press, 1999) 8.

Chapter 2

Frank Merriwell at Yale: The Football Hero as Masculine Center

There can be little doubt that football and American masculinity have been inseparably linked since the inception of the uniquely American game in the last half of the nineteenth century. As early as 1860, rural towns across the eastern United States featured football games in which men displayed their toughness, strength, skill, and general physical worth to other members of the town. However, in order to understand how men's concerns about their masculinity spurred the popularization of football, the rise of the football hero as a dominant behavioral center for young men and boys, and the subsequent development of football literature as a way of selling that center to those who craved it, it is necessary to illuminate the changing cultural conditions in America which ushered in dramatic alterations in accepted masculine norms around the turn of the century.

The young, middle-class boy of 1890 inherited a far different America than his father had entered in the 1850s. Spurred by post Civil War technological advances in communication, transportation, and mass production, America's economy, already irrevocably altered by the inception of the industrial revolution between 1780 and 1830, was again transformed through scientific innovation. Modern roads, railways, and telegraph lines connected burgeoning cities and opened new markets for industries that were beginning to capitalize on improved techniques of mass production. Goods formerly produced by individual artisans were now made in mass quantity by factories as "the individual craftsmanship of the ante-bellum years slowly yielded to large market dealers."[20] Farmers and individual artisans moved in mass to growing cities where factory jobs were plentiful. Not surprisingly, city populations exploded. By 1890 over 22,000,000 Americans called urban environments home, as compared with only 6,800,000 in 1860.[21] The population of New York City surged over 1,000,000 in 1890. Accompanying the masses was an industrial base growing with blinding speed. By 1870 the value of goods produced in New York totaled over $300 million. In the same year deposits in New York banks exceeded $250 million as industries and industrial workers flooded the city.[22] A consequence of these developments was that men who had once earned their "manhood" by supporting their families with distinct, usually physical, individual labor, now toiled namelessly on production lines. E. Anthony Rotundo writes that these changes in the workplace created a crisis for some men: "In the nineteenth century, middle-class men believed a true man was self-reliant. New structures of work did not support such a concept of manhood. Men expressed concern that public distinction and masterful independence were vanishing."[23] One of America's oldest masculine centers, the rugged individualist, was fading into the sunset along with the western frontier.

In addition to the drastic changes in economic conditions faced by men, social changes, especially in regard to changing gender roles, posed significant, often frightening challenges to the ways in which some men gained a sense of their own masculinity. Of special concern was the increasingly visible presence of women in the work world of the late 19th century. By 1900 women had made significant inroads into the previously male domain of the industrial workplace. Nearly 1,000,000 women were employed in factories by that year. Women especially concentrated in spinning and textile manufacturing, tobacco factories, boot and shoe factories, garment manufacturing and commercial laundries. Technological advances such as the telephone and the typewriter brought women jobs as operators and in clerical positions. In addition, women comprised the majority of schoolteachers by the end of the century. As Julia Kirk Blackwelder reminds us in Angela Howard Zophy's *Handbook of Women's History*, the Industrial Revolution completely changed the nature of work for women in the United States. While few women worked professionally outside the home in 1800, one-fifth of all women were wage earners by 1900.[24]

To be sure, it would be more than another half-century before women would hold positions of power, but their mere presence was enough to inspire fears of "feminized" men. As Michael Kimmel explains male trepidation of the "New Woman:" "She was an avowed feminist who asserted her autonomy in the world of men. [With her] the stage was set for a crisis in masculinity. Men felt besieged by social breakdown and crisis as the familiar routes to manhood became either washed out or road blocked."[25] Not only were men forced into competing for lower level jobs with women (thus equating their worth to that of women), but men were also forced to alter their language, smooth their rough, boyish behaviors, and exhibit a more formal politeness. As Rotundo writes, "Spittoons disappeared soon after women arrived. Now a man had to be genteel with his language at work as well as at home; ... the subjective reality for men was that their workplace was not masculine in the same sense that it was."[26] If female presence on the job didn't change the behaviors of all men, it certainly made significant numbers of them feel uncomfortable and altered the certainty of the notion that the workplace functioned as an exclusively male arena for the proving and achievement of manliness. The workplace would, of course, remain an important masculine proving ground, but increased women's entry into previously male turf was another blow to men's ability to make meaning of their lives by succeeding in the world of work.

Of even more concern to many middle-class men was the increasing amount of control women had over religious, educational, and domestic affairs and the power this gave women over the development of young boys. In the eighteenth century, most men and women worked at home, where men held significant control over the domestic sphere and the upbringing of their sons. The father role as a center of meaning was strictly defined in patriarchal terms. The Industrial Revolution created industries that took men away from the home both physically and mentally, leaving women in charge of their sons. As Mark Carnes confirms: "The transformation of gender roles and household responsibility greatly influenced child rearing patterns. One consequence was the physical separation of men from the home. Women assumed the duties of child rearing as their special vocation."[27] Women were able to extend their influence beyond the home, however, through their increasing involvement in the field of public education. By 1890 two out of every three public school teachers were women who "attempted to order the classroom through the power of love."[28] In addition, women dominated church congregations by the end of the century. Protestant women outnumbered men by at least a two-to-one margin, and their feminine presence was both highly influential and disturbing to men. Justin Dewy Fulton, a Baptist, summed up men's resentment against female control of religion:

> Within, in her lowest spiritual form, as the ruling spirit she inspires, and sometimes writes the sermons. Without, as the bulk of his congregation, she watches over [the minister's] orthodoxy, verifies his texts, visits his schools, and harasses his sick ... The preacher who thunders so defiantly against spiritual foes, is trembling all the time beneath the critical eye that is watching him with so merciless an accuracy of his texts. Impelled, guided, censured by women, we can hardly wonder if, in nine cases out of ten, the parson turns woman himself.[29]

This fear of feminization and feminized boys was of intense interest to men, who began "challenging female sovereignty over the moral instruction of boys" at the end of the 19th century.[30] Many middle-class men resented "woman's increasingly dominant role in religion and the moral authority it conferred upon their actions within the home."[31] Prominent men such as Theodore Roosevelt lamented the supposedly weak, pallid condition of American boys, and called for the development of a heartier, tougher, more vital brand of boy: "We need the iron qualities that must go with true manhood. We need resolution, courage, indominatable will, ... power. If we shrink from the hard contest ... stronger peoples will win domination of the world."[32] Part of this triumph would clearly have to be gained by liberating boys from the feminizing influence of women. Business, religious, and political leaders such as

Oliver Wendell Holmes, Jr. reaffirmed the traditional sentiment that "Woman is the mother, the ideal of unselfishness; man is the breadwinner and the fighter."[33]

Other social and cultural leaders echoed Holmes' sentiments. In *The Bostonians*, novelist Henry James used Basil Ransom to warn America of the necessity for reconditioning American boys away from the civilizing influences of women and toward a more virile, atavistic, physical type of masculinity: "The whole generation is womanized; it's a feminine, nervous, hysterical, chattering, canting age … which, if we don't look out, will usher in a reign of mediocrity, of the feeblest that has ever been."[34] His brother, psychologist and social critic William James, went so far as to call for the creation of a peacetime youth army, whose purpose would be to toughen boys, preparing them for the world's competition by getting "the childishness knocked out of them."[35]

Many men sought to regain control of boy's masculine construction by encouraging a "primitive" masculinity, characterized by aggression, physicality, competition, unbridled emotion and fighting. This, of course, was an attempt to resurrect a certain type of masculine identity that harked back to the ancients, but more recently to the Civil War hero, the cowboy, the explorer, and all manner of rugged individualists, and looked forward to the corporate warrior. Termed "He-man" masculinity by scholar David Pugh in his *Sons of Liberty* (1983), it was reincarnated to address male fears and bolster men's confidence around the turn of the century; it successfully reinvented the older, dominant masculine codes that had flourished for much of the nineteenth century. This was not a center based on being a strong father, an independent frontiersman or artisan who lived by his own code and labor, a military hero, a Christian servant of God, or a professional man. It had elements of those centers, to be sure, but it was based on conquest, the conquest of a number of "others."[36]

A premium was put on activities in which a boy could exercise his supposedly natural, animalistic passions and test his ability to survive brutal conditions, overcome pain, and display physical courage. Fighting, for instance, was encouraged and looked upon by fathers as a chance for their sons to prove their manhood. The popularity of boxing reached an all-time high, and novels such as Jack London's *The Game* celebrated male virility and power over highly submissive women and other male warriors. In his *The Manly Art: A History of Bare-Knuckle Prize Fighting in America*, Elliot Gorn writes that "by the last half of the nineteenth century, power obsessed many American males. Fascination with prowess was stimulated in part by fears that modern living rendered males intellectually and emotionally impotent. Men emphasized the importance of physical vigor because they were terrified of losing it."[37] As Rotundo points out, this masculinity of conquest not only revolved around power over women, but around power over other men as well, power that would supposedly translate into financial success in business or politics. It was common thinking that the more masculine the boy, the greater his chance of competing and winning in the adult world of work: "Bourgeois Northerners did more than endorse interpersonal violence. Students at Phillips-Exeter Academy were urged to 'plunge into it with bare fists and wits as your only weapons.' The fight was seen as an emblem for developing character, a means to manliness."[38]

Perhaps the most concerted attempt by men to gain exclusive control over maleness in the last half of the nineteenth century came in the popularization of fraternal lodges. By 1896 nearly five and half million of America's nineteen million adult men belonged to a fraternal order. The Odd Fellows had 810,000 members, while the Freemasons (750,000), the Knights of Pythias (475,000), the Red Men (165,000) and hundreds of other orders enjoyed huge memberships. These organizations served primarily to provide men with an exclusive male refuge in which masculine values and norms common to the group were recreated through dramatic initiation rituals. Carnes writes that "Lodges served as a 'spiritual oasis' in a rapidly changing and increasingly heterogeneous world. The eclectic religious motifs underscored values common to all members ... [and] the ceremonies articulated prevailing middle-class norms."[39] All lodge rituals reaffirmed patriarchal power. For instance, the Freemasons conducted an initiation rite whereby the young boy was "transformed" into a man by being symbolically killed by receiving mock sword wounds in both his left and right breast. Once the boy born of woman was dead, he was then reborn through an elaborate series of ancient incantations and patriarchal rituals which culminated in his rebirth through the power of his male brethren. He was then "fit to move in the company of men."[40] Other rituals, such as chariot races based on the one in *Ben Hur*, physical contests or mock battles, celebrated male power and a masculine code based at once on solidarity, brotherhood, competition, physical conquest, and the maintenance of male power, all values that members wanted to associate with themselves and each other in order to affirm their own potency and power in a changing outside world. As Carnes writes, "The orders were exclusively masculine institutions."[41] They were developed as an attempt to address the psychological needs of many American men who participated in the rituals "because they shared similar concerns about gender."[42] If Christianity was a once workable center for some men that had now been co-opted by women, the fraternal lodge became a new spiritual haven that jibed nicely with the reigning paradigm of conquest.

In any event, the lodge movement certainly celebrated a type of primitive masculinity which developed in response to cultural changes late in nineteenth century America. Lodges, however, were only one institutional attempt to regulate and codify boys' behaviors so as to bolster male power and self-esteem by redefining separate gender spheres and creating male space in which masculine traits that would specially qualify men (and disqualify women) for powerful adult roles could be nurtured. Kimmel sums up the situation:

> The separation of boys from girls became a kind of mania. Men were wary of the feminizing clutches of mothers and teachers, whose refined civility would be the undoing of American masculinity. If boys were provided with a place away from women, then they would surely become the real men required by industrial capitalism.[43]

But where could this space be carved out? No wars were being waged. The school, the home, and the church were dominated by women, and the workplace was increasingly populated by females. One of the most prominent new arenas of male cultural space was the athletic field, a world apart from mothers, sisters, and sweethearts, where men could learn to develop newly emphasized masculine traits under the tutelage of other men. As Michael Messner recounts:

> With boys being raised and taught by women, it was feared that men were becoming too soft and feminized. The rapid rise and expansion of organized sport during this era can be interpreted as the creation of a homo-social institution which served to counter men's fears of feminization, [a place] where true manliness could be instilled in boys.[44]

Athletics would thus become a significant and exclusive male sphere, where men could reclaim from women the power to mold boys.

In particular, the masculinity of conquest, with its emphasis on physicality, courage under fire, pain, brutal aggressiveness, and intense competition, in addition to corporate teamwork and leadership, lent itself to the gridiron, where the primal, tough, quasi-militaristic characteristics of football were thought to be a perfect testing ground for manliness. For the spectacular rise of football as privileged masculine space on university campuses late in the nineteenth century was due not only to the sport's appeal to college men, but also to the alumni of American colleges who wanted a game that would make their sons into men. As Kevin White confirms, "The controlled violence of football in these years was representative also of the rise of primitivism"as a prevailing philosophy among prominent men who, having served in the Civil War, feared that their sons would become feminized and weak without a masculine testing ground of their own.[45]

The first intercollegiate football game was played in 1876 and featured Rutgers defeating Princeton 6-4. By the turn of the century, college football had gained a substantial audience. A Thanksgiving Day game between Yale and Princeton drew 50,000 people, and all college games in 1911 attracted over 20,000,000 spectators.[46] Traditional rivalry games, such as those between Harvard and Yale, garnered a great deal of press coverage as early as 1900. The game's media coverage was at once romantic, mythic, and heroic, featuring glorious descriptions of idyllic young men fighting for the honor of their university, and by extension, their social class. It was, in part, this romanticized coverage that helped to spread the game's popularity. As Michael Oriard writes:

> ... the sensational reporting of games brought football to the attention of a huge audience ... The daily press in New York had an impact on college football in the 1880's and 1890's greater than the effect on pro football in the 1950's and 1960's. The daily newspaper press 'created' college football, transforming an extracurricular activity into a national spectacle.[47]

Not surprisingly, sports publications and popular magazines like *Tip Top Weekly* spawned football literature in the form of short serials as a highly profitable maneuver intended to capitalize on men's need for a masculine center of meaning, and thus, maximize the magazine's own circulation and profit. It was for that reason that the most prominent, early football serial, the Frank Merriwell saga, was born in 1896. The segments chronicled the romantic adventures of Yale's top gridiron great and sold 500,000 copies at the height of their popularity.[48] Eventually, the serial episodes were put into popular juvenile novels.

While many of our most recognizable football narratives (movies and novels) would be produced much later in the twentieth century, the Merriwell books, which are highly representative of the large number of juvenile narratives which characterized football literature until well after World War II, became significant cultural symbols because they attempted to market football as an ideal stage upon which privileged masculine traits could be developed and displayed. Of course, the Merriwell books were primarily designed to make money, but, in order to do this, editors knew that they would have to give boys and parents a masculine role model whom they would like, a newly established masculine center that would align with male needs. Oriard affirms that "the penny-paper serial taught a huge audience to read football as a powerful cultural text."[49] This was the indirect function and crucial literary significance of early football fiction. It reflected a new role model, the football hero, that coincided with a masculine center based on conquest, power, male spirituality, and raw individualism within a corporate structure.

Gilbert Patten's *Frank Merriwell Returns to Yale* (1905) is typical of all of the Merriwell sagas in that it is simply a series of theatrical scenes, each of which showcases particular facets of Merriwell's masculinity, a masculinity widely admired and coveted by the turn-of-the-century male audience. The opening scene sets the tone for the book by establishing Merriwell's startling mix of athletic skill, intelligence, and upright character. In this instance, Merriwell's friend, Page, attempts to embarrass the hero by locking him in an old fireplace in his new apartment. Never one to panic, Merriwell displays his raw physical ability by climbing the slick stone of the fireplace with the intention of extricating himself through the chimney. Half way up, however, Merriwell hears his math professor talking to a colleague. Frank quickly surmises that the professor's voice must be carrying through a vent. Although it takes every bit of his strength to hold onto the wall without making a noise to give himself away, Merriwell manages to hang on long enough to overhear Professor Babbitt's plan to give Merriwell's class a surprise math test. The special aim of the test is to trip up Merriwell, who, according to the professor, is "a scamp," who gets "marks with fair standing [while he] spends most of his time with athletics and skylarking."[50] Merriwell scampers up the chimney and back into the apartment in time to see the astonished look on the face of Page, who "got up looking very sheepish" at seeing that Merriwell had found a way out of the chimney.

Not only has Merriwell demonstrated the physical agility and cool head that would become a staple of the football hero, but he also finds out about the math test. Displaying a keen mind, Merriwell, always aware of his limitations, deduces that, since the test is designed to trip him up, it must deal exclusively with his weakness. Merriwell's friends are skeptical, but they believe in Frank's leadership abilities: "It was not difficult to persuade his closest friends to join him in studying hard on one topic. They were so in the habit of following his lead that they were willing to take their chances if Merriwell was." Frank then organizes a study group and saves his friends, all of whom pass the test.[51]

Still, Merriwell isn't out of danger. An enemy who is jealous of his athletic and academic ability places a "cheat-sheet" on Frank's desk, making it look as though he was cheating. Suddenly, Frank is faced with the pressure of being expelled unless he can prove his innocence. Disdaining panic, Merriwell affirms his innocence and his hatred for dishonest behavior:

> Frank held his head high ... with nothing on his face to indicate his true feelings. The thought of disgrace was hard to bear, but a conscience of absolute innocence gave him strength ... 'I don't intend to be browbeaten and insulted in this and leap out into the darkness.' [Still], Frank was unflappable. 'If you have any accusation to make against me, you can lay it before the faculty.'[52]

With everyone sure that he will be expelled, Merriwell deduces what has happened and sets a successful trap for the enemy student who framed him. Of course, his friends and Yale administrators are amazed by his cool brilliance under fire, and especially thankful for his innocence. As the dean of Yale says to Frank, "I was never so relieved in my life, Merriwell; for if it had been proven that you had done this thing, I am afraid that I should have lost all faith in students.[53]

Thus, the reader sees in the opening chapter the formation of a masculine center that, to some degree, still holds sway in American schools across the land Merriwell will embody mental toughness and courage, but he will also recapture for boys such traditionally masculine virtues as honesty and fair play. However, these gentlemanly qualities are tempered by physical prowess, an ability to handle adversity and an uncanny intellectual power consisting mostly of an unusual adeptness to think clearly under pressure. These traits, especially the primitive aspects of Merriwell's physicality, jibed well with contemporary masculine needs, recreating exciting myths about raw, male power, which men wanted boys to read.

As Pugh confirms, the Merriwell novels, like other male literature of the day, "provided an important psychological function by vicariously satisfying the long-held urge among some men to assert their masculine dominance."[54] Sportswriter Wendell Hazen expressed the sentiments of his generation in 1945: "Patten was the man who took me through prep school, who took me through college, who taught me the wonders of football and the fine many habits of courage, honesty and perseverance."[55]

Once Merriwell establishes himself as the "natural leader" at Yale, he must display his masculine worth by physically distinguishing himself as both an athlete and a fighter. For, in addition to his cerebral alacrity and steady nerves, Merriwell is above all a physical being, a dangerous he-man capable both of dealing out and accepting physical punishment. Like Merriwell, the he-man "embodies a powerful virility" and defines "through acts of prowess who he is in a complex world."[56] As captain of the intercollegiate team, Merriwell proves his individual strength and courage in an all-Ivy competition in New York City. When gamblers sidetrack the team's star tug-o-war anchor, Higgins, and get him drunk, Merriwell rushes to the rescue. Motivated by the thought that a newspaper scandal would destroy the university's honor, Frank single-handedly tracks down and pummels the gamblers. As Patten writes:

> Frank leaped from the doorway and caught the fellow a terrible blow on the side of the face. The attack was unexpected and sudden ... and Frank struck again. He was never so aroused and blows fell like rain on the [gambler's] face and chest. The others closed in, but Frank beat them off vigorously, striking without mercy.[57]

Having taught the gamblers a physical lesson, Merriwell, anxious for the success of Yale in every possible event and [desirous] to keep this thing from becoming public, then turns his attention to foil their plan to win big money by betting on Princeton against a weakened Yale squad in the tug o' war. To that end, Merriwell insists on taking position as Yale's anchor. As Patten writes, even though he was dreadfully undersized for the position, Merriwell "knew that the credit of Yale depended upon the good showing at the intercollegiate games."[58] Frank responds to the enormity of the occasion with he-man bravado that almost reminds the reader of such legendary heroes as Natty Bumppo or Davy Crockett. As he says to his teammates, "If you can think of anybody in the college more qualified than I bring him on."[59]

In the style of the old frontier hero, Merriwell gamely installs himself at the end of the Yale rope. The undersized hero is immediately forced to give ground almost to the point of losing because of Princeton's superior strength. The fans "left their seats ... and began to chant" for Merriwell to call for the "all out pull," but Frank exhibits his individual heroism by ignoring their doubting, derisive comments. As he continues to give ground, Merriwell hatches a plan under pressure. With his strength nearly sapped, Merriwell carefully waits until the fatigued Princeton crew is off-balance after a hard pull designed to finish off the Yale squad; he then issues the forceful order to pull. Princeton is caught unprepared and Yale is able to pull off an unbelievable victory. Patten describes the results of Merriwell's strategy: "Merriwell knew the instant the Princeton men had exerted all the force of which they were capable. The Princeton anchor was taken completely by surprise and the Princeton team was pulled completely off their cleats by the victorious sons of Yale."[60]

Highlighted here is Merriwell's ability to use his rugged athletic skill and individual savvy to pull victory from the clutches of a sure defeat. Just as significant is his use of mythical masculine traits to uphold the winning, untarnished reputation that Yale men wanted to associate with their alma mater and that most men wanted to associate with their gender. This masculine heroism that combined intelligence and moral character with romantic, frontier aggression and physicality allowed Patten's readers to transcend their own limitations in an increasingly complex world. Merriwell became the ideal masculine role model, the ultimate athletic hero. As Christian Messenger writes, "Frank is the boy with the greatest physical prowess and he carries the day in any situation, a convention which hardly resembles the plight of adolescent impotence in a world of authority."[61] He is the "stuff of legend because he was dreamed up [to be] his day's ideal of symbolic action and performance, a larger than life, heroic type that both the isolated farm boy and the street-wise city boy could identify with."[62] In short, he was the embodiment of mythical male power with which many young men, and several older ones, wanted to associate themselves.

Another element integral to the he-man side of Merriwell's masculinity that endeared the Yale gridder to male audiences was his willingness to confront danger and even death without flinching. Danger, to coin the cliché, is Merriwell's business. For example, when Merriwell is struck by a car and severely injured, the Pi Gamma society, into which he is being initiated, tells Frank that it will accept him without his suffering through the dangerous initiation tests. Merriwell, of course, refuses to take the easy way out, opting instead to endure each hazing activity. When the society men blindfold and shove him off a bridge into deep, freezing water twenty feet below, Merriwell, unlike several of the initiates, refuses to shirk from the danger. As Patten describes the scene:

> There was not one of the juniors who would have relished the dive if he had his eyes open and been dressed for the occasion, but it is quite another thing to be bound and blindfolded above a rushing current and leap out into the darkness. [Still], Frank was perfectly cool through it all.[63]

Merriwell, as the athletic hero, "is the one who does the extraordinary thing, and he does it alone."[64] It was this kind of romantic, fearless individualism that pleased a turn-of-the-century male audience that was so concerned with instilling this center of meaning in its boys. As Pugh argues, the football hero may not have actually been part of the lives of late nineteenth century audiences, "but [the reader] could read about [him] and gain a vicarious satisfaction in doing so."[65] Judging from the aforementioned sales figures of the Merriwell installments, that is apparently just what male audiences did with the Merriwell books.

The remainder of the novel is simply a sequence of similar scenes charged with Frank's hyper-masculinity. Merriwell continues to seek out and confront danger, overcome impossible odds, and defeat various enemies. At one point he refuses to back down from a duel to the death with a southern aristocrat named Marline. Merriwell had bested Marline for the starting halfback position on the Yale eleven, stinging the honor of the proud South Carolinian. Marline insists that Merriwell is a coward and challenges him to a duel with sabers. Despising all forms of cowardice, Merriwell fights the duel despite knowing that Marline is a skilled swordsman. As Frank says, "Marline has acknowledged publicly that he is no fighter with his fists. I'd seem a bully if I hit him. I have to meet him in a duel."[66] Naturally, Merriwell's bravery, coolness under fire, and raw physical ability allow him to disarm Marline. As Patten describes the gallant hero:

> Frank was calm and confident. His nerves were under admirable control. Merriwell gave ground. He knew that Marline was dangerous, for he had flung discretion to the wind and was exposing himself in all ways. Frank did not wish to wound Marline, only humble him. He had remarkable control of himself and waited for his chance. In time, he twisted the sword from Marline's hand. Marline covered his eyes with his hands, his whole body quivering.[67]

Despite being wounded, Frank allows Marline to live, offering his hand graciously in friendship as he tempers his aggression with mercy. This type of fair-minded dispensation of justice is an integral part of the athletic hero's masculine code. Never does Merriwell allow others, even the school or the law, to fight his battles for him or to determine the quality of his anger or mercy. As such, he becomes a new embodiment of the old American frontier hero, the Bumppo or Crockett, who transcends institutional control to implement his own system of justice.

Indeed, Frank's masculine identity rests on his ability to deal firmly but fairly with his enemies. For instance, when Merriwell identifies the man who hit him with the car as a gambler who had once tried to fix a Yale football game, Frank devises a stylish revenge. His fellow society members kidnap Miller, telling him that Frank is dead, and that, as Merriwell's society mates, they must exact revenge by killing the perpetrator of their friend's death. They proceed to blindfold Miller, leading him through several torturous hours of harassment during which he thinks he is going to die at any time. The Pi Gammas taunt Miller after drugging him with a harmless substance that he believes is poison: "He ought to have his head chopped off; I should rather think it would be better to boil him in a vat ... and burn him alive on the marshes; ... I think a hanging is best."[68]

Eventually, they convince him that Merriwell has been resurrected by a mysterious potion. The revived hero then grants the half-crazed Miller a pardon. Not surprisingly, Miller decides to leave town. Merriwell has entertainingly exacted a type of self-fashioned, frontier justice for the wrong done him without actually hurting anyone. Of course, this romantic, cowboy image conformed with the rugged masculine style with which many men wanted to identify around 1900 after the closing of the actual frontier. For as Pugh writes of characters like Merriwell, "If he makes it as a man, he must do so by himself; the virtues of manliness cannot be realized any other way."[69]

Once Merriwell has displayed the idyllic masculine traits that make him worthy of being an athletic hero, he is ready to take center stage in what is usually the climax of a Merriwell novel, the football game with Harvard. Here, Patten effectively uses football as a privileged, masculine stage upon which a type of empowering, albeit romanticized masculinity is recreated for readers in the person of the nearly supernatural Merriwell. As Oriard indicates, the idea that the football field was a proving ground for manliness was not lost on boys early in the twentieth century. By the late 1880s Thanksgiving Day football games were drawing thousands of spectators. The 1887 game between Harvard and Yale drew over 20,000 fans.[70] Not surprisingly, newspaper coverage exploded. By the latter half of the 1880s every major newspaper in the country and several sporting journals covered football, often devoting several pages to big games. The *Boston Herald*, for instance, focused six of its pages on the 1897 Harvard-Yale game, the coverage replete with romantic descriptions and pictures of rugged, physically dominant men thrashing heroically about the gridiron. By 1900 every city paper from Boston to Portland, Oregon was giving in-depth coverage to college heroes on both a local and national level. As Oriard writes, "Football became one arena for validating masculinity; for those who watched and who read about the games in the daily newspaper, football generated dramatic narratives in which ... ideas about manliness were a major theme."[71] Patten's audience, then, would have understood the significance of gridiron heroics to men and boys, and it is thus on the gridiron that all of Merriwell's manly attributes are fully displayed for public adulation.

It had been a down year for Yale because Merriwell, much to the chagrin of Yale supporters, had decided not to play on the eleven. Merriwell desperately wanted to play all year, but had promised his sweetheart, Inza, that he would not play. Inza exacts the promise from Frank to test his loyalty to her and his sense of honor and integrity dictate that he must keep his promise to the girl he loves. With only one game left, his classmates call Frank a traitor for not defending the honor of Yale against the hated Crimson. He overhears one classmate say that "Merriwell is a dead duck at Yale. He'll never count for anything anymore. He's universally rated a coward.'[72] This is more than Frank can stand. He exclaims, "For the honor of Yale I will do anything. It's for old Yale – dear old Yale. She has no right to ask so much. I will play."[73]

When Merriwell arrives at Cambridge for the big game, even the staunchest Yalies don't believe the young hero can save the day against the bigger, faster Harvard squad. However, Merriwell's tenacity keeps the game close. Patten's description of Merriwell saving a touchdown for Yale is typical of the romantic flavor of the gridiron climax:

> Harvard called on Benjamin [who] had the speed of the wind and a clear field before him. Every Yale spectator held his breath. Where is Yale? What chance has she to stop the little fellow with wings on his feet? Three seconds

of suspense seemed like three hours of torture. A Yale man was after Benjamin; the slightest slip would bring failure, [but] it seemed like the Yale man had springs in his legs. He closed in and flung himself at the little fellow. Down went Benjamin within three yards of the Yale line. Twenty men piled upon tackler and tackled. Deep down beneath the mass was Frank Merriwell; he had stopped a sure touchdown.[74]

Eventually, however, Harvard does manage to score, while Yale cannot move the ball. Frank is brutalized by the huge Harvard line and sustains several painful injuries each time he runs the ball. Patten painted the scene emotionally:

The Harvard crowd cheered and sang songs. They hugged, tooted horns and indulged in wild antics. The sons of Old Eli were dolefully silent. They had seen Yale fling herself upon Harvard time after time and rebound as a ball rebounds from a solid wall, and their hearts were weak within them.[75]

Still, Merriwell, as always, displays both his physical courage and mental acuity to help save the day. Frank has insisted on running inside at the strength of the Harvard line despite the persistent catcalls and criticisms from the stands. As the clock ticks down, the bloodied Merriwell shows why he had willingly absorbed punishment by running the same play all day. Expecting Merriwell to run the ball inside, the Harvard defense is caught unawares when he fakes a run up the middle and then darts outside around the end. Before the Crimson can react, Merriwell is being mobbed in the end zone by teammates, fellow students and alumni:

It was Merriwell making a last desperate effort for a touchdown. One by one the interferers were flung aside. Three men flung themselves down on him like famished wolves. The ten thousand people gasped in astonishment, scarcely able to believe what they saw. It did not seem like Merriwell slackened, and he went forward carrying three men on his back and shoulders. They could not drag him down and, with all of them on his back, he carried the ball across the goal line. It was a Yale touchdown, the most wonderful touchdown ever made on a football field. Oh, how the Yale men shrieked! They were like human beings gone mad. They were crazed with their admiration for the man who had done the trick. They longed to do him every honor ... Merriwell kicked the goal. Yale had won. All of Merriwell's admirers rushed upon the field to fight for a look at him.[76]

In one small window of time in the confined space of the gridiron, Merriwell has displayed courage, the willingness to take and give pain, the ability to think under pressure, the desire to compete despite a woman's pleas, to win against all odds, and above all, the willingness to defend Yale's honor in the manner of the rugged, mythical heroes of American folklore. Of course, in doing this, Merriwell has exhibited the perfect blend of masculine behaviors required of Patten's male audience. For the middle-class man enveloped by a new, mechanized, corporate age, Merriwell displays intelligence, integrity, and an ability to lead and manage groups of men in a manner that was both stylish and effective. For upper class men fearful of "feminization," Merriwell's patriotism, bolstered by hearty, he-man, masculine traits, inspired confidence that the masculine development of their sons, as well as traditional gender roles and separate gender spheres, would be institutionally maintained through male power. As Oriard writes:

> Football's rite of passage ... wed romantic neoprimitivism to the requirements of a modern technocracy, implicitly acknowledging rival models of masculinity but denying their incongruity ... Football's cultural power derived in large part from this collision of the modern and the antimodern ... Football could represent a union of the physical and the mental that was difficult for men to find in modern America."[77]

Thus, the football hero "built manly Christian character" for moralists, "validated the managerial manliness of the corporate executive" for the middle class and "regenerated the potency of a ruling class fearful of growing effete."[78] Certainly, Frank Merriwell the football hero was just what President Roosevelt ordered, just what the fragile, complex masculine needs of white, middle and upper-class men called for.

In addition to having Frank save the day and reaffirm his masculine worth, Patten rounds out Frank's romantic portrayal by having him win the unquestioning devotion of the beautiful girl. When Frank decides to play against Harvard, Inza says that she will never see him again. At the beginning of the game she exclaims, "Oh, he is a wonderful player. But he cares more for his college than me. I'll never speak to him."[79] However, when she watches Merriwell play so gallantly, she can't help cheering: "It's Frank. He has put life into the Yale men. He must win now ... he will ... If he is beaten, I'm sure that I will never speak to him again."[80] She realizes she loves and needs Frank, and her stereotypical portrayal as helpless and fully dependent on Merriwell clearly reinforces the traditional gender roles that many men desperately wanted to maintain. For while Frank is smart, tough, and cool under pressure, Inza is shallow and so simple that she doesn't realize until the end that her friend, whose fiancé plays for Harvard, has tricked her into asking Frank not to play for Yale so that Harvard might win. The final scene, in which she sobbingly pledges undying loyalty to Frank, is truly revealing: "I have been a foolish girl. I had no right to bind you. You know what is best, always, and after this you shall have your own way in everything."[81] Thus, at game's end, traditional gender roles are maintained and the idyllic Merriwell wins the game and the girl.

Thus, from the opening scene in which Merriwell preserves the academic integrity of the all-male university, to the intercollegiate competition where he preserves the public honor of the school, to the football game where he defends the athletic honor of Yale, to the treatment of Inza where he preserves traditional gender sphere, Merriwell's masculine display has been directed toward erecting a bold new center of masculine meaning, the football hero. In doing so, he worked to preserve a status quo in which white, middle-class men controlled academic, social, political, spiritual, and economic arenas. This seems to be the function of Patten's athletic hero, who, in the final scene, preserves the Yale class system by first punching out a freshman bully who had been pummeling second class students in an attempt to boost his fellow freshman past the sophomores in the competition to get into Yale societies, and then brutalizing an entire gang of toughs that resented his athletic success. Of course, "Merriwell had bested his enemies ... almost single-handed ...

a feat that was sure to add to his record."[82]

To the very end, Frank has directed his efforts toward establishing a template of behavior designed to preserve social class and gender distinctions by proving the superiority of an aggressive and powerful masculine code, a code based on a combination of mental acuity, strong nerves, and physical toughness that was best nurtured in masculine spaces such as the gridiron. Of course, he as steadfastly dedicated himself to winning victories for and proving the moral superiority of Yale (his "country"), which, after all, is what those fearful of feminization, industrialization, immigration, and the apparent deterioration of an America they had always dominated wanted of their young men. The football hero as a center for meaning seemed to gather up the best of other faltering centers such as rugged individualism, the Christian leader, the family man, the business mogul, and the war hero, and blend them together in the perfect package for men and boys at the time.

It is significant that Patten chose football, popularized largely as a game meant to bolster a faltering sense of manhood among late nineteenth-century men, as the principle stage upon which to have Merriwell develop and display his masculine behavior. Of course, other contemporary authors attempted to achieve similar goals with football narratives. As Messenger writes, "By the time Patten had established the convention of the boy athlete in series story, other authors came forth with their Merriwell imitations."[83]

These included several Ralph Henry Barbour novels. Among these were *The Halfback* (1899), which features a boy winning acceptance and earning his manhood through football exploits at a new school. Barbour's novels not only depict the hero's struggle to prove himself on the gridiron, they also involve the hero overcoming a character flaw. *Left End Edwards* (1914) is the story of a young man overcoming his habit of dodging blame for his mistakes by making excuses. In *Fullback Foster*, the hero must conquer his penchant for snobbery. Of course, in every case the hero does overcome the flaw to become the worthy athletic hero.

In Owen Johnson's nostalgic *Stover At Yale* (1912), the athletic hero displays a familiar sense of loyalty to his school, but, while he must win great victories for Yale and display superior athletic prowess, Johnson emphasizes the importance of his ethical development as well. Dink Stover, for instance, becomes his own man by rejecting the radical demands of students who want to bypass authority in order to abolish the society system at Yale and by standing up for the democratic values he comes to believe in. In *Princeton Stories* (1895), *The Adventures of a Freshman* (1899) and *Girl and the Game* (1905) and *Other College Stories* (1908), Jesse Lynch Williams echoes a similar narrative pattern featuring the importance of both physical and ethical development in the football hero.

As late as 1960, this Merriwellian formula was still dominating football narratives. John R. Tunis' *Iron Duke* (1938), Philip Harkins' *Touchdown Twins* (1947), William Heyliger's *Top Lineman* (1943), Leonard Burgess' *One Man Backfield* (1953), and William Heuman's *Second String Hero* (1959) all represent the influential legacy of Patten's hero. Of course, as cultural conditions changed, so did the manner and exploits of the football hero. For instance, the college films of the forties and fifties were created against the background of the great depression, World War II, the philosophic strain of the failure of modernism, and other social changes that took place between the twenties and 1960. Tired of poverty, war, and philosophic uncertainty, America retreated to familiar centers such as the athletic hero. Naturally, they touched up the Merriwell model a bit, but the result was largely the same. The result is best represented by films like *Knute Rockne: All American* (1941), which celebrated the masculine virility and strength of character of the legendary Notre Dame coach, a Swedish immigrant who fought his way to the top. In this film, the hero cultivates a uniquely American identity through football, "the most wonderful game in the world." Through hard work and a determined spirit, Knute rises from humble beginnings to stardom as a player and then coach of Notre Dame. In a time when America was at war with Adolf Hitler and his racist policies, the movie reminded audiences that the United States really is the land of the free, where men from all backgrounds can forge a new life. In addition, when Americans were suffering economically because of the depression and then the war, Knute's long but determined journey from working as a mail room clerk to becoming the legendary football coach reaffirmed the ideal of the American dream. Hard work, tenaciousness, inventiveness, and good character would lead to success no matter where one started his journey. Naturally, many of the Merriwellian staples such as physical prowess, mental acuity, and grace under pressure are still evident, but Rockne's story was very much a tale for the 1940s as opposed to the first quarter of the century.

To be sure, there were a few novels which diverged sharply from the pattern. Charles Ferguson's *Pigskin* (1929) and Millard Lampell's *The Hero* (1949) were two forerunners of the next generation of "adult" football novels. Both deal with college football as an economic institution in which the football hero is not only less than ideal, but is actually a dishonest ringer who accepts money and other special favors for his services. While this image is undoubtedly much more realistic than the Merriwellian story, it was the latter, dedicated to preserving a rugged, proud, mythic, individualistic masculine code that was being increasingly threatened by political, economic, and social changes, which utterly dominated the first sixty years of football literature. Until the 1960's when the civil rights movement, the Vietnam War, abrupt social change, and the ascendancy of postmodernism signaled another period of crisis for American men, "Frank Merriwell's sons" remained the prototypes of the football hero. As Oriard writes, "It was Patten who discovered the formula that made Frank Merriwell one of the most widely known heroes in all of American fiction … Athletics defined the spirit of a new time, and Merriwell became the new hero."[84] The football hero provided a masculine center that was well defined and much beloved, but neither he nor it could last.

Notes

[20] John Rickards Betts, *America's Sporting Heritage: 1850-1950* (Reading, MA: Addison-Wesley, 1974) 75.

[21] Betts 174.

[22] Marvin Adelman, *A Sporting Time* (Chicago: University of Illinois Press, 1986) 22.

[23] Rotundo 248.

[24] Angela Howard Zophy, *Handbook of Women's History* (New York: Garland Reference Library, 1990) 694.

[25] Harry Brod, ed., *The Making of Masculinity: The New Men's Studies* (New York: Routledge, 1992) 142.

[26] Rotundo 250.

[27] Marc C. Carnes, *Secret Ritual Manhood in Victorian America* (New Haven, CT: Yale University Press, 1989) 110.

[28] Carnes 112.

[29] Carnes 78.

[30] Rotundo 234.

[31] Carnes 78.

[32] Rotundo 235.

[33] Rotundo 227.

[34] Henry James, *The Bostonians* (New York: Macmillan and Co., 1886) 100.

[35] Rotundo 234.

[36] David Pugh, *Sons of Liberty: The Masculine Mind in Nineteenth Century America* (Westport, CT: Greenwood Press, 1983) 11.

[37] Eliot Gorn, *The Manly Art: Bare-Knuckle Prize Fighting in America* (Ithaca, NY: Cornell University Press, 1986) 193.

[38] Rotundo 225.

[39] Carnes 3.

[40] Carnes 12.

[41] Carnes 14.

[42] Carnes 15.

[43] Brod 149.

[44] Michael Messner, *Power at Play* (Boston: Beacon Press, 1992) 14.

[45] Kevin White, *The First Sexual Revolution: The Emergence of Male Heterosexuality in America* (New York: New York University Press, 1993), 11.

[46] Betty Spears and Richard Swanson, eds., *History of Sport and Physical Education in the United States* (Dubuque, IA: William C. Brown Publishers, 1988) 226.

[47] Michael Oriard, *Reading Football: How the Popular Press Created an American Spectacle* (Chapel Hill, NC: University of North Carolina Press, 1993), 58, 89.

[48] Christian Messenger, *Sport and the Spirit of Play in American Fiction: Hawthorne to Faulkner* (New York: Columbia University Press, 1981) 171.

[49] Oriard, *Reading Football* 89.

[50] Gilbert Patten, *Frank Merriwell Returns To Yale* (New York: Macmillan, 1905) 20.

[51] Patten 34.

[52] Patten 43.

[53] Patten 62.

[54] Pugh 131.

[55] Messenger 172.

[56] Pugh 132.

[57] Patten 80.

[58] Patten 88.

[59] Patten 116.

[60] Patten 122.

[61] Messenger 166.

[62] Wiley Umphlett, *The Achievement of American Sports Literature* (Toronto: Associated University Press, 1991) 32.

[63] Patten 155.

[64] Pugh 144.

[65] Pugh 143.

50

[66] Patten 294.

[67] Patten 305.

[68] Patten 180.

[69] Pugh 139.

[70] Oriard, *Reading Football* 128.

[71] Oriard, *Reading Football* 191.

[72] Patten 233.

[73] Patten 237.

[74] Patten 239.

[75] Patten 242.

[76] Patten 247.

[77] Oriard, *Reading Football* 200.

[78] Oriard, *Reading Football* 213.

[79] Patten 242.

[80] Patten 243.

[81] Patten 307.

[82] Patten 336.

[83] Messenger 171.

[84] Michael Oriard, *Dreaming of Heroes: American Sports Fiction 1868-1980* (Chicago: Nelson-Hall, 1982) 29.

Chapter 3
Frank DeFord's *Everybody's All-American*:
The Failure of the Football Hero as Masculine Center

Like *Frank Merriwell Returns To Yale*, Frank DeFord's novel, *Everybody's All-American*, a work written in the 1980s as a considered reflection on the 1950s, depicts football as a privileged masculine arena which, because of its dominant position on the American social landscape, exerts a powerful influence on young boys and men to adhere to a prevailing masculine center embodied by the football hero. The subject of the novel is Gavin Grey, and we watch him rise and fall because of his identification with the code of the football hero in the deep South during the 1950s. DeFord makes it clear that, like all masculine centers, the football hero, unbeknownst to its youngest and most passionate adherents, is more fragile than it seems, and is dependent for its stability on a complex, highly-fluid weave of economic, political, social, and religious attitudes in any given society. Deford's depiction of Grey's ascension and decline signifies the second step in the process of masculinity: the exposure of an established center as the result of changing personal and cultural circumstances.

An examination of 1950s football literature reveals that the Merriwellian type football hero of juvenile novels was still going strong even a half-century after its inception, apparently filling a deep need in part of America's collective psyche. Dick Friendlich's *Left End Scott* (1955), William Gault's *Bruce Benedict, Halfback* (1957), Philip Harkins' *Breakaway Back* (1959), William Heuman's *Left End Luisetti* (1958), and the prolific Wilfred McCormick's *Five Yards To Glory* (1959) are only a few of the books that represent the hundreds of 1950s juvenile football novels which depict the romantic adventures of an American golden boy as he displays strong, manly characteristics to overcome seemingly invincible obstacles and lead his team to victory.[85] Despite the passage of fifty years and two world wars, this football hero is eerily like Frank Merriwell. He usually has the respect of most students and adults, has a beautiful, faithful girl on his arm and generally exhibits values which are consistent with those of the community. Even football films of the late forties and early fifties, such as *Good News* (1947), *The Spirit of West Point* (1947), *Jim Thorpe: All-American* (1951), *Hold That Line* (1952), *The All-American* (1953), and *Crazy Legs* (1953), reflected a football hero whose identity seemed stable, pristine.[86] The question that has to be answered is, why? Why was the football hero of Victorian America still going strong, albeit with a few cultural modifications, free from censure or exposure at mid-century?

In part, these characters in these books and films reflect the relatively conservative nature of 1950s America, a country which, in the days which preceded the volatile 1960s, desperately wanted to believe in heroes, especially young, clean-cut, status-quo upholding boys fighting for their schools on the gridiron. That the slightly modified Frank Merriwell type football hero could still thrive as a masculine center in the 1950s becomes less of a mystery when one considers the psychological state of the country at mid-century. To put it bluntly, Americans were fatigued after two decades of hardship. Perhaps it all started on a fateful Monday in October of 1929 when the stock market collapsed and sent the economy into a free-fall that wouldn't begin to correct itself until well into the mid-forties. To say the least, the crash caught Americans by surprise. World War I they had been told was the war to end all wars, and it was followed by a decade of economic expansion nearly unparalleled in the history of the nation. The roaring twenties brought reckless speculation fueled by unrealistic optimism. When it all came crashing down, Americans were stunned and then stupefied. There was seemingly nothing to do to remedy the situation. Businesses failed, fortunes large and small evaporated, and jobs disappeared. Land lost much of its value and farms went under in record numbers nationwide. By 1935, nearly a third of American men were unemployed and a considerable percentage of America's middle class, so prosperous in the 1920s, has slipped into poverty or near-poverty.[87]

The depression ran headlong into World War II. When the Japanese bombed Pearl Harbor on December 7, 1941, it was the first time since the British invaded the country in the War of 1812 that the United States had been attacked at home in such aggressive fashion by a foreign power. Americans had never felt more vulnerable. With a shaky economy and a military largely unprepared to fight Axis aggression, Americans knew they were in for an uphill battle. Of course, that is exactly what the second world war turned out to be. From 1941-1945, the United States lost over 400,000 soldiers in combat. Many families lost fathers, sons, and brothers in the conflict, making the rationing and belt-tightening taking place on the homefront that much tougher to endure. Until the tide began to turn in early 1944, it was not altogether clear that the sacrifices would be worth it. Day in and day out Americans lived with doubt, not knowing if family members fighting overseas were still alive, not knowing if they were going to be able to make ends meet at home, not knowing if the Allies could win the war. By the time the war finally did wind down in the spring of 1945, Americans were tired.[88]

Winning the war was no doubt a relief, but the respite was to be short-lived. It is true that the war jump-started the economy and that, with Europe in shambles, America would emerge as the world's dominant industrial power in the 1950s. Still, by 1949, the nation would be at war again, this time in Korea fighting a "conflict" whose aims at first seemed much less defined and important than those of the second world war. The perils of the Cold War would become all too clear, however, as the conflict in Korea wore on with American troops taking heavy losses. The Soviet Union emerged as the world's other superpower, supplied China and North Korea with aid, and made it clear that Russian communism did not intend to play second-fiddle to American democracy. Then, in 1953, the unthinkable happened. The United States signed a peace treaty and went home, leaving South Korea at the mercy of the communists. American military might had come up against ill-equipped and underfunded North Korean forces, and the world's best hope for defending freedom against authoritarianism had lost. The United States also lost another 54,000 soldiers and a great deal of its self-confidence.[89]

Events of the 1950s would only exacerbate the nation's fears. The defeat at the hands of the communist forces in the Korean War ignited a sense of vulnerability in Americans that would grow to near hysteria as the decade progressed. Senator Joseph McCarthy of Wisconsin became the symbol for the country's obsession with communism when he asserted in 1950 that the government was replete with communist sympathizers. McCarthy leveled his charges at, of all places, a meeting of the Ohio County Women's Republican Club in Wheeling, West Virginia; still, the atmosphere was so charged that even this little spark set the nation ablaze. Panic struck the nation; paranoia proved to be a powerful lens, making it seem like there were communists everywhere. Congress investigated government officials, college professors, businessmen, writers, actors, and anyone else whose activities seemed "un-American." The Keefauver hearings and the trial of the Hollywood Ten gripped the nation. Thousands of innocent people would lose their careers, and even after McCarthy was exposed as an opportunistic phony, the Red Scare lost little steam. In 1957, the Soviets launched Sputnik, proving that it had the rocket power to send missiles into American airspace. Shortly after, a U.S. attempt to launch a similar satellite failed spectacularly, causing Americans to feel that the country had fallen behind in science and in the space race, leaving it vulnerable to atomic attack. The Cold War had settled over the United States, and Americans showed their trepidation by making a new industry, the selling of bomb-shelters, a going concern.[90]

As if a long economic depression, the sacrifices made to win World War II, the loss in Korea, and the ensuing threats to national security, both real and imagined, weren't enough, Americans also found themselves adrift in a sea of significant cultural changes that would have been somewhat unsettling even in the best of times. It is, of course, true that Americans enjoyed the affordable cars, televisions, and houses available to them in the 1950s, but the problem was that it was all happening so fast. The proliferation of automobiles caused the landscape to change quickly. Gas stations, motels, and fast food restaurants began to dot roads across the country. Americans began to travel like never before and the possibilities surrounding adventures on the American road excited many people. However, such romanticism also came to be associated with Jack Kerouak's *On The Road*, whose vision called for a bohemian search for spiritual vision that frightened American parents. Television offered "wholesome" entertainment such as *Leave It to Beaver* and *Ozzie and Harriet*, but it ran on advertising money, and the American home suffered the intrusion of hucksters of all kinds of new and improved merchandise. One such product was the record-player, a device which symbolized freedom to American teens, but was a tad scary for their parents. For the music their kids were listening to had changed. Gone was the big band sound that defined the forties, replaced by the hip-twisting, pelvis-thrusting, hard-driving lyrics of Elvis Presley, and stunningly, the fast-paced sound of what would be called "race music." White parents used to the mores of Jim Crow America saw their kids listening to Chuck Berry, Little Richard, and Fats Domino, and they were not ready for it. Neither did they know what to make of the 1954 Supreme Court decision, *Brown v. The Board of Education*, which called for the integration of American schools, or of the continuing integration of professional and college sports teams, or of growing talk about civil rights. It seemed as though every change that one could see as an advance had its scary side hovering just out of reach of the public discourse. Affordable, mass-produced homes, such as those made famous by Bill Levitt, allowed thousands of Americans to own their own home, but they were also ugly, offered little privacy, and bespoke of a numbing conformity that would give rise to powerful novels like Sloan Wilson's *The Man in the Grey Flannel Suit* (1955), which not only bemoaned fifties conformity, but also the loss of individualism felt by men in an ever-growing corporate jungle. The nuclear family promised bliss for women, but Grace Metalious' *Peyton Place* (1956) and Betty Friedan's *The Feminine Mystique* (1963) showed that women, too, were growing restless. Even fun and harmless inventions like the drive-in movie brought films like *The Wild One* (1953) and *Rebel Without a Cause* (1955) that to parents reflected a growing unrest in their children that they could sense under the calm veneer of fifties' confidence. These same theaters would combine with the automobile to provide a perfect setting for young people to engage in sexual antics that would become all the more worrisome for parents when Gregory Pincus introduced the birth control pill to American consumers in the early sixties. There was prosperity and progress to be sure, but there was also a feeling that something was afoot behind the progress that had to be suppressed.[91]

In short, the technology and cultural transformations that would lay the groundwork for the upheavals of the 1960s were being experienced by Americans who, in the 1950s, were already tired after two decades of depression, war, and loss. Psychologically fatigued and unprepared to handle the cultural complexities brewing underneath their newfound success, Americans sought literary and visual representations that soothed their fears. In the face of latent racial tension, some loved *The Lone Ranger* all the more. Good old Tonto. Mickey Spillane's *Mike Hammer* novels featured a hard-edged detective who often battered communist sympathizers. Television shows like *Leave It to Beaver, Ozzie and Harriet*, and *Donna Reed* featured female protagonists who were so happily dedicated to Victorian notions of femininity that the women's movement of the sixties would have seemed an impossibility to loyal viewers. Consciously or unconsciously, Americans craved "safe" artistic portrayals that would help them recover from a difficult past and promise them protection from an uncertain future. This desire is what made the football hero viable in the 1950s.

In *Everybody's All-American*, Gavin Grey is not only a football hero; he is a southern football hero. DeFord gives the first five pages of the novel to the subject of narrator Donnie McClure's recent book, Confederate general Jeb Stuart, a man who in the eyes of his countrymen embodied all of the heroic, romantic qualities that the Civil War South wanted to believe about itself. Deford continually juxtaposes

Stuart with Gavin Grey throughout the novel, and the reader quickly sees that the citizens of North Carolina will not let Grey be Grey anymore than they would let Stuart be Stuart. To them, he is the Grey Ghost, the larger than life hero who embodies the pride of Carolina; one look at the University of North Carolina campus lets the reader know that Grey is the biggest thing to hit the state in years. McClure, now a prominent professor with a wonderful family, opens the novel by admitting that "there has never been anything so exciting in my life as the weekend ... that I visited Gavin Grey at Chapel Hill. I still measure all my other memories by it."[92] We then witness the Ghost's exploits against Duke through the eyes of young Donnie McClure. What we see is much of what we saw in the Frank Merriwell novels: daring runs, improbable catches, and many brilliant touchdowns. According to Donnie, "Gavin was famous, handsome and heroic, and in no ways a man or a real person."[93] Indeed, he was known to all as Everybody's All-American, and everyone stares in quiet awe when he walks across campus. Clearly, Gavin is something bigger than life, almost an ethereal hero.

Having grounded the reader in Ghost mythology, DeFord explores the sources of his heroic status, allowing us to watch Grey on the North Carolina campus where he is clearly king if not God himself. Every student, it seems, attends the games; the band performs choreographed songs, the highlight of which is "Dixie," the crowd sings lustily, and even the shrill voices of excited cheerleaders are drowned out by the students who cheer "Ghost! Ghost! Ghost!" The divisiveness and rebellion that would characterize the 1960s is still a decade away, as is the beginning of the New South with its commitment to civil rights, technology, and commercialism, and the focus of the entire, unified campus is the championship football team. At center stage is Gavin Grey, who walks though a fraternity party like a king being flanked and regaled by his loyal subjects. His queen, Babs Rogers, stands in pristine beauty at his side as the crowd continues to roar, "Ghost! Ghost! Ghost!" There is little doubt that football carries great significance here, where "all stopped whatever it was they were doing as soon as Gavin walked through the door" with his girl on his arm.[94] Grey and

58

Babs waving to their cheering onlookers has left an indelible print on Donnie's mind, and the reader knows that for a moment in time in pre-civil rights North Carolina the Ghost and his blueberry queen reigned supreme.

It is important to understand that DeFord takes the time to show the reader that once he is the Ghost, Grey's identity will never be his own again; it is something bestowed upon him by his society; he has the talent, but they have the power to make him the Ghost. DeFord utilizes several scenes to show how Grey's admiring, Southern society conspired to cement his status and identity as the Ghost, their hero who represented the triumph of their values and way of life, even though that way of life was largely composed of romantic visions of a time long passed. As Donnie says, "It was the last of the good old days, although we did not know it at the time."[95] Even Donnie, Gavin's cousin, can barely talk the first time he visits the Ghost on the Carolina campus; Gavin warns him not to pay attention to the Everybody's All-American stuff, assuring him that he is still the same person he always was, but the reader can see that Gavin's society has made him different. It has made him into a Southern hero. When he opens the door to leave, he must make his way through a crowd of boys who have been waiting at the door just to catch a glimpse of the hero. All white, clean-cut, middle-class, Southern boys, they collectively gasp in disbelief at the sight of Gavin. He is one of them, the hero who symbolizes their own potential greatness. As Mrs. Stringfellow, a ninety-five year old lady who as a young girl had once met her hero, Jeb Stuart, said to a newspaper reporter: "All my born days, I never thought these old eyes of mine would see such a sight as General Stuart riding to Spotsylvania, and they didn't, either, till two weeks ago when I saw The Grey Ghost in the second half against State."[96]

At a postgame victory party, the fraternity men stop everything to cheer for Gavin when he appears at the door. Their cheers, of course, are the omnipresent "Ghost! Ghost! Ghost!" that reverberate through the first half of the book. Gavin tries to hold onto his identity as a person, but he can't escape "the antebellum dream he was raised on."[97] Early in the novel, Gavin is still aware that he is a person apart from the Ghost, but the community continues to encourage him to play the role of the legend until his entire identity becomes one with the Ghost. At the party, the young men rally around him and stare open-mouthed as their boy recounts his game-day heroics. He is their ideal, everything that they would like to be. The girls can hardly get near him, because the boys gather around him wherever he goes, fawning over him as if they hoped a little bit of the Ghost's magic might fall off onto them. Lawrence, his best friend, is one of many North Carolina men to emotionally admit in public how much they love "the Ghost man." Even when he goes to the bathroom, an admirer screams, "Wait'll I tell folks back home I took a piss with the Grey Ghost hisself."[98] Exasperated, Gavin sarcastically tries to bring the man back down to reality, but the undaunted fan is so pleased that he ignores the slight. After all, he has peed with the Ghost. Even when attached to the urinal, Gavin is the Ghost, their man of mythical qualities who they have chosen as an exemplar of Southern manhood (above successful politicians, bankers, lawyers, or doctors) because of his ability to bring greater glory to North Carolina on the gridiron, perhaps the most highly valued and visible masculine stage in the nation at the time.

As the viewer begins to fully understand the importance of Gavin's college football exploits to some Americans, and to many North Carolinians, the significance of Gavin's identity as the Ghost comes into focus. Having established, however, that he is the ultimate manly hero whose place atop the social hierarchy is unquestioned, DeFord begins to delve further into the sources of Grey's legendary status, allowing the hero to display the characteristics that have so enthralled his community.

The key to his status is the football gridiron, where several of his most admired traits are put on display every Saturday. For the game against Clemson, everyone who is anyone in the state has flooded Keenan Stadium, and the reader can almost feel all 50,000 people in attendance chanting in unison, "Ghost, Ghost, Ghost." Responding to their call, the man who is "number twenty-five in your programs and number one in your heart" executes a dazzling touchdown run in which he fakes out several Tiger defenders, runs over another, and outraces the rest to the end zone to secure the victory and a trip to the Sugar Bowl. All the fans rise as one to cheer his amazing physical exploits, while the players mob Grey. As it gets late in the game, the cheers of "Ghost, Ghost, Ghost" resonate across the stadium like a praise hymn. It is almost a solemn occasion. Donnie actually starts to cry. The final gun sounds and everyone storms the field; opposing players try to clasp Gavin's hand, but it is hard to get close to him. For "the children, who had crashed down onto the field, swarmed upon him, reaching out just to touch, calling to him, repeating his name, ... witnessing a legend in their own time."[99]

The Tar Heel faithful are worried in the days prior to the Sugar Bowl, but their fears soon turn to tears of joy as the Tar Heels dominate the opposition behind the Ghost's brilliant running. Grey loves the pressure, and on play after play he delivers amazing runs and improbable catches that captivate his loving audience. He is cool and calm amidst his throng of nervous retainers, adding humility to his list of virtues. Again, thousands of amazed worshipers chant, "Ghost, Ghost, Ghost," as Grey is carried off the field one last time as a collegiate player. As Donnie says, "the tumult was exceeded only by the emotion. Even Babs could not contain herself. She cried in her seat, just as the judge [a family friend] cried before his television set ... Gavin's countenance showed such peace amidst all this exaltation."[100] At this point, Gavin has at least unconsciously embraced his identity as the Ghost, and he is at his height as a football hero.

Of course, as football hero, Grey does much more than simply play football. In addition to his nearly supernatural prowess on the gridiron, Grey's superior masculinity hinges on his embodiment of social behaviors with which many Southerners wanted to identify. Among those are his generosity, his sense of fair play, and particularly, his willingness to sacrifice himself for his admirers. Never is this more evident than at the aforementioned fraternity party at which a girl named Caroline Cross catches on fire as the result of a bizarre accident. Everyone is so shocked that they just stand and watch her scream and jump out of her seat. Those who understand what is happening panic and seem to freeze under pressure. Only

Gavin Grey recognizes Cross' plight and rushes to her rescue. According to Donnie, "He dashed to an alcove and from the wall grabbed one of those little red fire extinguishers ... how Gavin knew it was there I'll never understand. In three more steps he was on Caroline Cross." The flames had nearly engulfed her dress and were ready to burn her body. "In that last moment, Gavin ripped open the extinguisher tab and fired a burst of foam upon her, killing the fire dead."[101] Gavin then pulls down the fiery drapes, "thrusting his hand into the very heart of the flames," and puts out the rest of the fire. When every spark has been extinguished, Grey realizes that he is on top of Cross. Every bit the gentlemen, he says "Excuse me, m'am," and then walks out into the night, his legend having grown even larger.[102]

If Grey was a gentleman on the order of old-time southern chivalry, he was also an unlikely diplomat. In a time in which racial relations were strained and the civil rights movement which would scare southern whites to death was just over the horizon, Grey also had the ability to preserve traditional racial relations between blacks and whites. When he learns that a local legend, Narvel Blue, lives nearby, Grey jumps at the chance to meet him. Blue was the top black player in North Carolina, who couldn't compete against Grey because of discriminatory laws preventing black players from attending white universities. Blue, who will eventually give up football and become a tremendously successful businessman and state senator in the New South, has heard of the Ghost and is eager to race him. Although, as Blue recognizes, the Ghost has nothing to gain from a race like this, Grey responds with a friendly smile: "I hear nobody can beat you in the open field. You want to run, let's race." While Lawrence greedily takes bets on the race, actually allowing Blue to bet not only his money but his car as well, Grey talks amicably with Blue, smoothly preserving socially imposed racial limits by maintaining a distant friendliness through their competition. When Grey wins the race, Blue is exasperated, but Gavin modestly apologizes for having the advantage of being in training. Blue's friends and relatives are in a somber mood, but Grey will not allow Blue to lose his possessions. A few days later, he returns to "coloredtown" with a brand new Impala that local dealer Bolling Keily had tried to give him in exchange for publicity. He gives it to Blue. Everyone is overwhelmed with joy. It is no wonder that one older black lady says to him "Mister Ghost, I do declare, would you mind if an old colored lady kissed you?"[103] Such displays of modesty, fair play, and generosity help to cement his legendary status. Of course, the reader cannot help but notice Grey's ability to conduct racial relations in a time of growing racial tension between blacks and whites in the South. Grey is friendly with Blue, but does not befriend him. He races Blue as an equal, but he wins. He is kind to the African-American restaurant owners who host them after the race and will not allow them to be exploited. However, Grey, as the white hero, remains in control. It is he who decides how the winnings will be used and how justice will be dispensed. Clearly, equality and fairness are hinted at, but distance and white superiority are maintained in what must have been an acceptable illusion of racial harmony for whites, an illusion embodied by Grey as a white hero.

Another of Grey's admired traits is his unwillingness to corrupt amateur athletics by marketing his name or taking gifts for himself. Whenever he sees Bolling Kiely coming his way, his usual reaction is to send Donnie or Babs to deal with him: "I'm sorry, Donnie. I just don't like that man. Oh, yeah. I ... seen him kissin' the coaches asses before."[104] At a country club dinner, Gavin rebuffs Kiely's offer of a new car and is offended when Kiely tries to sweet-talk him into accepting it. He is, however, more offended that his friends think he doesn't understand what Kiely is trying to do: "You think I'm just a dumb jockstrap who couldn't know how to handle this. That's what-all you think?"[105] When Donnie and Babs assure Gavin that he won't get in trouble, the hero reacts with a kind but firm answer: "It would be common. See, if I got caught, nothin' would happen to me. But they could take the whole season away from the team ... and that would be common."[106] He then displays his cleverness and creativity by concocting the plan to have Kiely give the car to Narvel Blue. While this display of honesty and honorable, gentlemanly behavior helps bolster his heroic status, it also shows that his sense of self is completely inbedded in the Ghost. As he tells Babs, the Ghost stands for something, and he must be protected. Gavin knows that he is a chosen Southern hero in the mold of Confederate generals such as Robert E. Lee or Stonewall Jackson. To him Southern honor is entrusted, and he accepts the responsibility.

Perhaps the most crucial element in Grey's successful adoption of the Ghost as his identity is the fact that Babs, the most beautiful Southern belle on the campus, worships him as a kind of deity. She follows him dutifully as he is honored at different parties and even allows him to arrange a chaperone (Donnie) for her so that she will never be unattended. Babs attends the Women's College in Greensboro, but is content to leave school without graduating. After all, what she is actually majoring in is Gavin Grey. She simply functions to reinforce Grey's identity as the mythical Ghost, who naturally gets the ravishing, loyal blueberry queen. Like Gavin, she plays a role in the ante-bellum tradition. He is the Confederate hero of romantic lore, while she is the nearly angelic Southern "lady" who stands by her man. Of course, these traditional roles of hero and heroine were especially revered by white Southerners in the 1950s as they struggled to hold on to their traditions and regional identity in the face of modern economic, social, and political realities.

That Babs' deportment as the traditional belle is central to the Ghost's fragile, masculine identity is made clear by DeFord, who devotes several scenes to the depiction of their relationship. For instance, when Babs finds out that she won't be able to compete for the Miss America pageant if she marries Gavin, she cries desperately on his shoulder. As a lady, it is her duty to allow her man to solve her problems, acting helpless so that he may feel strong. Gavin is mindful of his duty as well and gallantly tells her that they can postpone the wedding until after the pageant. Of course, Babs issues the appropriate response, saying that she will not hear of it and that she is willing to give up everything for him. Babs is so devoted to him that she even consents to the age-old double standard which allows Grey to enjoy the sexual pleasures of "punchboards," while she remains a virgin. Babs just doesn't care. All she wants to do is be Mrs. Gavin Grey.

Indeed, every scene in which one sees Babs at the University of North Carolina involves her looking out for Gavin's reputation. Even at the Clemson game, she says to Donnie, "I do hope I look all right, Donnie. It just wouldn't do for Gavin Grey's girl not to look attractive."[107] When the Ghost cries after saving Caroline Cross from the fire, Babs tells Donnie, "don't y'all ever tell anybody about Gavin in the car last night."[108] After Grey and Donnie sneak off from a family affair that Babs has arranged so that Gavin can race Narvel Blue, Babs reprimands her soon to be husband, but allows herself to be quieted by this explanation: "Babsie, I love you, but I ain't gonna make you say no to me again till we're married. I don't gotta. I beat Narvel Blue tonight, and you ain't never gonna know what that was like till you sleep with me. And you can wait all you want, sweetheart, because I got mine."[109] The reader isn't sure whether it's 1850 or 1950. Only a few nights after the Sugar Bowl and a few days before he will become the number one draft pick in the NFL, Grey, the Ghost, soaks in the teary forgiveness of his adoring fiancée, knowing that he is the idol of millions. According to Southern mythology, Grey is now the perfect example of what a man should be. There are no wars in which Southern manliness can be displayed, so he cannot be a military figure in the mode of a Lee or a Jackson. But Grey does display the physical, mental, and mythical characteristics of the hero in the next best arena, the gridiron. On the football field, the Ghost exhibits physical prowess, courage, and dominance. Off the field, he is fair, kind, and sensitive. In addition, his demeanor reaffirms traditional Southern attitudes toward gender and race that many whites, both male and female, wanted to maintain. He has it all, everything the football hero is supposed to have, everything he needs to keep his identity as the Ghost intact. Only time will reveal the fragility and dangerous nature of this identity. As the Judge says to Donnie regarding Grey: "Understand what Gavin Grey is to us. He is Alexander, Robin Hood, General Washington; he is ... Jeb Stuart. He is Sergeant York."[110]

The problem, of course, is that this masculine center of identity can't last. It simply can't withstand the test of time. Gavin will grow old and his skills will erode;

times will change and the South will in the end have to abandon its mythology for the realities of modern capitalism and a democratic nation finally trying to live up to its promises to all of its citizens. As the Judge says to Donnie, "Ideally, HE-roes should die at their heroic peak. Once you hit that heroic peak, it must be all downhill."[111] Even Donnie, on attending the year-end awards ceremony, realizes that the time of the Grey Ghost has passed. Babs admits that "all the games are over."[112] Gavin would, of course, go on to have a fantastic professional career, but he could only be the Ghost on the campus of the University of North Carolina in 1954. Only then were the conditions right to let the football hero in the form of the Ghost function as a workable center for a man's identity. As times changed, the good folks of North Carolina would forget about the Ghost. They just wouldn't need that kind of hero anymore. For Grey, there was nowhere to go but down.

The next time the reader sees Grey in a football uniform is in Canada, where the Toronto franchise has made him a better offer than the Washington Redskins of the NFL. Grey is a great player, but he is not the Ghost. After three years, he goes to the Redskins and the reader watches him trudge through the mist and mud of RFK Stadium in Washington, D.C., where he starts for the last place Redskins. The damp, cynical, small crowds make for a stunning contrast to the passionate throngs at North Carolina. Gavin gets crunched time and again into the muddy turf. The fans boo lustily and Grey's face winces with pain. Gone are the bright lights of Keenan Stadium, the cheerleaders, the bands, and the glory. This is especially true for Babs, who finds out that there is no one to admire her in the players' wives section. She is with the rest of the women, most of whom used to be queens of something, but are now just players' wives.

The opening scenes of the book had been filled with examples of the chivalric Grey "taking care" of Babs with highly symbolic, though practically meaningless gestures. Gavin might put his coat around her, comfort her, assure her that she is his girl no matter what. As the blueberry queen, her dependence on him is central to his masculine identity. However, once she is removed from the North Carolina campus, she can no longer be a queen, and she becomes increasingly dissatisfied with her new, less glamorous role as a player's wife and as a mother. Depressed, she tells Donnie: "Some women love children. And I'm not that kind of lady."[113] She understands that she has been sentenced to spending all of her time doing things that don't complete her: being a good player's wife and a mother. She admits to feeling like a piece of furniture, like a dining-room set. She wants to do the twist with Donnie when he comes to visit, and she makes him go skinny-dipping with her. She is anxious to show him her body. She is a young girl trapped in roles she doesn't like, and she starts to see her husband as less than a splendid hero: "Players are all little boys. Who do you think is going to marry little boys? Little girls, that's who. And the little boys keep on playin' their games, and they give us little babies so that we little girls can keep on playin' with dolls."[114]

In many ways, Gavin is a little boy. His body will mature into a man's body, but inside he will always remain the football hero, the Grey Ghost. The more Babs realizes that she has to let go of the past if she is to grow as an individual, the more Gavin tries to hang onto the past. In this way his dependence on her is accentuated. The reader can see that he is heading for a crisis. For Babs is smart, young, and ambitious; she is starting to realize her worth as a person, not just as the Ghost's girl and the mother of his children. He, on the other hand, finds his joy only on the field, and the closer he gets to the end of his football life the more he clings to his identity as the Ghost. More and more, the reader watches Gavin apologize to his cross wife and seek consolation in her arms when he is afraid. For instance, after Lawrence, Gavin's best friend from college, loses all of the Ghost's life savings by gambling them away while he was supposed to be managing his restaurant, *The Grey Ghost Inn*, Gavin falls apart. He can't believe that Lawrence would do something like that to the Ghost; even after he is presented with undeniable proof that the mob killed Lawrence to avenge his gambling debts, he still thinks "it was some niggers" that did it.[115] While Babs faces the crisis head-on, Gavin merely buries his head in her chest and cries. Donnie, Babs, and even Lawrence know that the Ghost was gone, but Grey doesn't quite understand. It is as if he is lost in the waves of change; he can't get his head above the water long enough to rationally figure out what is happening to him, but he can feel it.

This emphasis on Gavin's desperate dependence on Babs is cleverly juxtaposed by DeFord with some of the defining moments of the 1960s. The reader is reminded of Neil Armstrong's moon landing, and thus of the fact that the world is getting smaller, moving inexorably toward a global village which will make the campus of North Carolina look terribly small. There are the election and assassination of President Kennedy, speeches by Martin Luther King, and civil rights marches in the South that not only mark the passage of time, but also symbolize a period of accelerated change in the lives of Southerners. There will be social upheaval, political turmoil, and rapid technological change. Most of all, however, the reader is reminded of the successful movements for racial and gender equity that drastically altered the socially ordained roles (and power) played by American men and women. These movements, which would eventually take a tenuous hold even in the South, would combine with Gavin's eroding physical skills to render the Ghost's chief functions obsolete.

Not surprisingly, Gavin and Babs' relationship does not escape the changing realities of their world. DeFord devotes several scenes to chronicling how the two gradually grow apart because of their contrasting responses to their new environment. Grey becomes an uninteresting character in many ways because he is so remarkably static. Though he claimed not to care about fame or attention when he had plenty of both in college, he nearly becomes addicted to both as he senses that his career is winding down. This becomes particularly evident when he sustains a serious injury late in his career. Grey maintains that he will come back better than ever, but DeFord uses Donnie, the Judge, and most importantly, Babs to let the reader know that the Ghost is in denial. The reader can sense that the Judge's prophecy that Grey's status as the Ghost "will be his burden" later in life is coming true.[116]

At the same time that Grey is regressing, Babs continues to come into her own. She is clearly a frustrated, overworked mother of four. The house is cluttered, and the once impeccable Babs now wears baggy jeans and old t-shirts. She is discontent, but Gavin doesn't seem to see or understand this. Perhaps her continued submission is so necessary to his identity of the football hero that he can't let himself notice. She expresses her frustration to Gavin, but he refuses to take her seriously. When Donnie comes to visit her, she revels in the fact that he talks to her about world events, politics, history, and economics. "Oh, Donnie, I've loved having you here. I've never talked like this to any man before." Donnie protests that surely she and Gavin must talk all the time, but Babs just laughs sarcastically: "Gavin and I talk about ... Gavin and me." Donnie tries to ease her evident pain by saying that most married people fall into a rut every now and again, but Babs refuses to do anything but look reality square in the face: "No, Donnie. I 'spect that's just me and Gavin."[117] As always, the Judge sums up the situation well: "In a very real way, Babs and Gavin married for the past, for autumn Saturday's gone. And that's an awful lot to overcome."[118]

Things get worse when Grey retires. He can't find anything to do with himself. He makes a sad attempt at a comeback, but fails in such pathetic fashion that everyone around him starts to pity him. He finally lands a job as an Assistant Pro at a local country club, where the owners give him the title of Vice President because they remember the Ghost from the good old days and don't want him to lose face in the community. Of course, they also covet his name and the legendary reputation he still enjoys in North Carolina. Indeed, many golfers at the club do enjoy playing with Grey, but his constant retelling of stories about past glory gradually turns him into a caricature. Meanwhile, Babs takes a job as Regional Manager for Narvel Blue's restaurant chain, Dreamers. Blue has made himself wealthy by buying several McDonald's franchises when they first came into the Carolinas. He had asked Grey to go in with him, but Grey, living in a romanticized Southern past, did not want the Ghost's name to be used for vulgar marketing purposes. Babs, on the other hand, is a startling success. She proves to be smart, resourceful, witty, clever, and an extremely hard worker. She only leaves Blue's company to take a managerial job for the company that owns the golf course where Gavin works. Babs does this so that she can be closer to Gavin; she still has hopes that her marriage can work, that Gavin can shed the Ghost and grow up. As the years go by, however, she realizes that he will always see himself as the legendary football hero; he will never be a man. She becomes entrusted to run the company; he drinks, plays golf, and retells the same stories to golfers who are less and less interested in who he was. She works out and keeps herself in shape; he smokes and drinks himself into an ashen, pudgy middle-aged man.

Babs does everything she can to help her husband find a place in a post-Ghost world, and she maintains faith that the relationship can be saved until they attend the ceremony for Gavin's induction into the Professional Football Hall of Fame. Ironically, the turning point for Babs comes during one of the few times in their married life when they are content. The focus is on Gavin as a football player and he is happy; Babs, confident because of her success in the business world, can now enjoy being a player's wife for a day; indeed, she is proud to be the wife of a hall-of-famer. They laugh and joke like they were in college, and for a moment it seems like they are, like they have gone back in time to a place where he can again be the football hero with an appreciative audience and she can be his queen. They make love in the afternoon and in the evening with a ferocity that makes Donnie and his wife, Karen, envious as they listen in awe in the next room. Yet, as Babs would relate to Donnie a few years later, it is what Gavin said to her after their love-making that made her finally understand that she had to leave the Ghost. Gavin says to her, "Wouldn't it be great if I still played football."[119] This is when Babs finally understands what so many others had long known. Her husband was the football hero, the Grey Ghost, and he would never be anything else as long as she, a centerpiece of his identity as the football hero, was still his possession. DeFord writes that Grey became increasingly "disconnected," but it is one of Grey's new golfing partners who has grown bored with his stories who says it best: "Jesus, I feel sort of sorry for the guy. He can't get out of 1954."[120]

By the end of the novel, Babs and Gavin are at opposite poles. One is tempted to say that they have changed positions, with Babs now being in the provider role. To some extent, this is true, but it implies that Babs now occupies some legendary, unrealistic place on the American landscape. That is far from the truth. For Babs has matured and she has a grounded, reasonable healthy view of who she is. The independent Babs is characterized by several qualities, one of which is an assertive brand of sexuality in which she is the subject, not the object. Gone is the simpering virgin of 1954; in her place is a woman who will no longer accept the old sexual double-standard that defined the South when she was growing up. This is evident as early as Gavin's retirement party from professional football. Gavin is whisked away by his fellow players to enjoy the favors of another "punchboard." Babs knows this, but she will no longer retire innocently to her home to let Gavin have all the fun. As she says to Donnie, "Dammit, it's my retirement too."[121] She then proceeds to seduce Donnie, who becomes the first man besides Gavin with whom she has been intimate. By the end of the novel, Babs has become even more aggressive. Gavin confronts her with charges of infidelity one night, and she looks him in the eye and says, "I was with a young guy last night, Gavin. I got a piece of ass last night."[122] Not only is she in control of her own body for the first time in her life, but she is financially independent as well. She has been making the lion's share of the money for years and is willing to accept financial responsibility for her kids, herself, and even for Gavin. As she tells Donnie, "I'll support him. He can keep the house … I've got a little place out there, a kitchenette, and I'm going to stay there, all by myself, loving it, until I figure out what to do"[123] She has always been physically beautiful, but the reader now sees that she is mature and beautiful in a deeper way as well. After all, she actually does all of this not just for herself, but also for her husband, whose refusal to grow has pushed her out of the football hero cocoon. As she says to him, "This is for *you*. I'm leaving for you. I stand for all the things you've lost. Maybe if you lost me too, it would make it easier."[124] Babs has grown and she has a benevolent self-confidence about her. As she modestly asserts: "I'm a very confidant woman. I only lost my youth. I didn't lose my beauty."[125]

On the other hand, Gavin's descent is painful to watch. Unable to let the past go, he "graces" Donnie with the opportunity to write his biography. Ever the good friend, Donnie tries to gracefully sidestep the project by telling his cousin that he has just signed a contract to write a book on Jeb Stuart. Gavin, however, is unrelenting; he is sure that the entire country will want to read about the Grey Ghost. Donnie, Babs, and Karen all wince and bite their tongue, knowing that not many would even remember Grey at this point but not wanting to hurt his fragile feelings. Things get worse when Gavin is fired from his job at the golf course. The new owners try to be nice to him, but Grey threatens them, arguing that if they let him go they will lose all of their business because people in North Carolina won't put up with such a show of disrespect to the Grey Ghost. The owners turn the other cheek for a while, but Gavin becomes increasingly belligerent. Finally, one of the owners, a young man from New York who knows little about the legend of the Ghost, blows up at him: "Do you really fucking think anybody's gonna give up a game of golf on their day off just because you helped beat East Cupcake U a hundred years ago? You really think anybody gives a rat's ass about old Mister Jockstrap?"[126] To this Gavin can say very little. Down deep, he knows it's true. Still, for all this, the saddest part of Grey's awakening to his own insignificance comes at the University of North Carolina's silver anniversary celebration for his 1954 championship team. It is clear that the people in the stands have little memory of the team; there is only a smattering of applause as the players are introduced at halftime. Gavin is introduced last and there is a huge ovation, but not for him; it is for the current Tar Heels who are returning to the field. Later, at a post-game dinner, most of the former players just treat Gavin as another player; they are nice to him, but he is not a hero. In fact, because he doesn't have a career to talk about and the other players have mostly gone on to fulfilling careers as lawyers, doctors, politicians, and businessmen, Gavin ends up alone for most of the evening. It is a pathetic scene. By the time it is Gavin's turn to speak, all he can do is stare dumbly out into the crowd, realizing that he is not only not The Grey Ghost anymore but that he is a kind of fossil who can't even join in conversations with his former teammates about current issues or events. After all, he has no idea what is happening in the real world. His world is the dream scape of 1954, where fans waved ostrich feathers when he scored touchdowns. "I thought they should have had some ostrich feathers to wave, didn't ya'll," he finally stammers.[127] The audience laughs politely. He mutters a few other incoherent remarks, leaving his friends with quizzical and then embarrassed looks. The Judge rescues him by quietly starting the old chant of "Ghost, Ghost, Ghost." It is kindly meant, but everyone who heard that same chant twenty-five years ago knows it is, like Gavin's life, a pale imitation of what was once full of energy and meaning. For Gavin Grey, the Grey Ghost, the football hero as a center of meaning has collapsed.

One of the dominant masculine forms in 1950s America, and especially in the South, was the football hero, and Frank DeFord's novel is an excellent depiction of the rise and fall of this center of meaning. When Gavin Grey was young, with great physical ability, his identity as the Ghost propelled him to great heights in a society which revered the football hero as a superior man. His public adherence to societal values such as honesty, amateurism, generosity, and fair play further cemented his legendary status in the deep South where many white Americans, alarmed by growing civil rights disturbances and critical press coverage among many other cultural changes, craved a hero who could earn them glory in a prestigious arena like college football while still reaffirming their traditional attitudes toward both race and gender. The fact that Babs played her socially sanctioned role as the dependent blueberry queen who lovingly submitted to his every whim solidified his identity as the Ghost, the man of ante-bellum, Southern legend whose physical prowess and traditional demeanor commanded the loyalty of a beautiful woman and the admiration of the society whose values he represented. He was a modern day Jeb Stuart, a pre-civil rights, southern Frank Merriwell. But the process of masculinity is unrelenting. As soon as a center is formed and sanctioned by any given group of people, it is cast on its inexorable journey toward exposure as a false center whose temporary stability is washed away in the torrents of societal change.

By 1980, Gavin's skills have deteriorated, and football is no longer viewed with such respect as an arena or field which produces the spectacle of an ideal man. As Donnie says to the Judge, "Football was a rite [of manhood in America]. It's changed one hundred and eighty degrees. Football is a painful exercise to be avoided. It's soccer in the suburbs, now."[128] In addition, values such as amateurism and the sexual double-standard are considered passe or embarrassingly quaint; athletes are expected to market themselves and women are liberated. Just as importantly, the South has slowly begun to change its collective attitudes on race, gender, and that which constitutes honorable behavior. The conditions which allowed Gavin to thrive in his fragile identity as the Ghost have disappeared and left him with only memories. He has no real friends, no skills, no direction, and an empty existence barely sustained by tired stories. His adherence to his identity as the Ghost has betrayed him and he commits the action of a desperate man. He sets his house on fire so as to kill both himself and Babs, a final attempt to keep her under his authority, to hold on to the Ghost. Babs escapes, but Grey allows himself to be engulfed by the flames. For him, suicide is preferable to living with no meaning.

Notes

[85] Donald L. Deardorff II, *Sports: A Reference Guide and Critical Commentary, 1980-1999* (Westport, CT: Greenwood Press, 2001)137-163.

[86] Deardorff 163-193.

[87] Robert McElvaine. *The Great Depression: America 1929-1941* (New York: Times Books, 1984) 162-182.

[88] Richard Schwartz. *The 1950s* (New York: Facts on File, 2003) 1-45.

[89] Schwartz 382-414.

[90] Kenneth D. Rose. *One Nation Underground: The Fallout Shelter in American Culture* (New York: New York University Press, 2001) 20-42.

[91] David Halberstam, *The Fifties* (New York: Ballantine, 1993) 456-486.

[92] Frank DeFord, *Everybody's All-American* (Cambridge, MA: DeCapo Press, 2004) 5.

[93] DeFord 6.

[94] DeFord 42.

[95] DeFord 9.

[96] DeFord 7.

[97] DeFord 40.

[98] DeFord 44.

[99] DeFord 31.

[100] DeFord 111.

[101] DeFord 46.

[102] DeFord 47.

[103] DeFord 59.

[104] DeFord 90.

[105] DeFord 91.

[106] DeFord 91.

[107] DeFord 29.

[108] DeFord 48.

[109] DeFord 76.

[110] DeFord 15.

[111] DeFord 98.

[112] DeFord 121.

[113] DeFord 175.

[114] DeFord 176.

[115] DeFord 190.

[116] DeFord 107.

[117] DeFord 141.

[118] DeFord 181.

[119] DeFord 320.

[120] DeFord 267.

[121] DeFord 214.

[122] DeFord 352.

[123] DeFord 351.

[124] DeFord 353.

[125] DeFord 317.

[126] DeFord 304.

[127] DeFord 336.

[128] DeFord 296.

Chapter 4

Don DeLillo's *End Zone*: Understanding Ironic Resistance

Like Frank DeFord, several fine American writers have penned fiction that exposes the football hero as being a false center. Works such as James Whitehead's *Joiner* (1971), Peter Gent's *North Dallas Forty* (1973), Bill Davis' play *Dancing in the End Zone* (1985), and Irwin Shaw's short story "The Eighty Yard Run" (1941) have something in common with *Everybody's All-American*. Despite being well-written, compelling pieces of literature, they don't offer an alternative center beyond resistance, beyond simply walking away from the game and the athletic system that produces the template of the football hero. Walking away is fine, but you have to have something to walk to. Ultimately, men want meaning more than anything else; they want to embrace a positive center, not just resist a negative one. None of these works moves beyond resistance to posit a stable, healthy center. Take *Everybody's All-American*, for example. By the end of the novel, Gavin Grey's former football playing friends are pictured as happy, well-adjusted bankers, lawyers, politicians, and businessmen; some, like Gavin, are husbands and fathers. However, DeFord doesn't develop any of these characters. He doesn't comment on the viability or stability of the various socially constructed centers that they have adopted after their football playing days. One is left with the impression that if one can just move beyond the faulty confines of the football hero, one will find contentment by embracing any of the many masculine alternatives that are just waiting for men to find them. Life experience tells us that this is not, in fact, the case. Masculinity is much more complicated. Why don't talented, thoughtful writers like DeFord, Whitehead, Gent, Davis, and Shaw offer an alternative beyond resistance to the flimsy center of the football hero? Don DeLillo shows us in *End Zone*.

Like other writers of his generation, DeLillo understands the destructiveness of the football hero as a masculine center. His main character, Gary Harkness, certainly knows that the world of football can hurt him. Even at the start of the novel, football has already occasioned horrible experiences for Gary at universities that temporarily cause him to give up the sport. It seems as though he has come unglued as the result of the sport's violence. Gary is fascinated by the word "MILITARIZE" which he sees on Army recruiting posters around his town and consistently feels that he is being programed through football. Unable to deal with the militaristic uniformity at Syracuse, he barricades himself in his room in order to hide from the coaches; numbed by the violent repetition of drills, he suffers a spiritual crisis at Penn State; when he accidentally kills a player in a game at Michigan State, he is so disturbed by the consequences of his violence that he vows to quit the game, which he feels is militarizing him to be a type of combative machine. Nevertheless, he always comes back to the game. As he says, "I discovered one simple truth. My life meant nothing without football."[129] The same is true for the rest of his teammates. They are all "exiles and outcasts," boys who have been drifting across the country's campuses, desperately looking for a sustainable identity on the gridiron.

DeLillo seems fascinated by his characters' reactions to their plight. Why, DeLillo asks, are these young men so drawn to football and its masculine imagery considering how hurt they have been by it in the past? DeLillo shows us that the answer lies in the person of head coach Emmitt "Big Bend" Creed. He promises his charges that at Logos College they will find the secrets to life, that they will find meaning rooted in something beyond the material forces on which they usually base their identities. In short, he promises them that they will find ultimate meaning, the Word. As running back Taft Robinson tells Gary:

He was part Satan, part Saint Francis. He offered nothing but work and pain. He'd whisper in my ear. He'd tell me he knew all of the secrets ... He'd tell me about the work, the pain, the sacrifice. What it might make of me. No time for nonessential things. We would deny ourselves. We would get right down to the bottom of it.[130]

Creed promises that both he and Logos will live up to their names, supplying the boys with a dominant code by which to live life. And this is what the boys so desperately want, a grand narrative that is ultimately stable because it is rooted in the Word. Creed himself is surrounded by mystery and legend. Creed establishes his authority through the mystery and legend that surrounds his background. According to Gary, he "was born in Texas, in a log cabin or a manger, depending on who you believe," and has allegedly won fame "for creating order out of chaos."[131] He has an aura about him, and these young men, though their attempts to find meaning as football heros in the past have met with disaster, are so desperate in their quest that they are ready to give it another try with Creed in the searing deserts of southwest Texas.

DeLillo admits that his novel is not about football; it is about language, "extreme places and extreme states of mind."[132] Nearly everyone there, the players, the professors, and the other students, are extreme in their attempts to find the Word, but the players are DeLillo's special focus. Indeed, the novel is full of unusual characters who are obsessed with stretching or breaking the boundaries of what is acceptable speech or behavior in order to find stability within their insulated world of the Logos football machine. Many of the Logos players are intellectuals whose complex phraseologies and insightful inquiries challenge the stereotype of the dumb jock. These players attempt to experiment with language either to separate themselves from the traditions and linguistic patterns which force them to conform to a harmful masculine template, or at least to find some sense of order and stability within that template. For example, Gary's roommate, Anatole Bloomberg, tries to completely separate himself from history and tradition, especially his Jewish heritage which makes him feel the weight of the guilt of being an "innocent victim." He says that "I am working myself up to the point where I can exist beyond guilt, beyond blood, beyond the ridiculous past."[133] Anatole goes so far as to condemn history and tradition as things which end in disastrous repetition:

History is no more accurate than prophecy. I reject the wrathful God of the Hebrews. I reject the Christian God of love and money. I reject heritage, background, tradition and birthright. These things merely slow the progress of the human race. They result in war and insanity, war and insanity, war and insanity.[134]

Anatole changes his name to EK Seventeen and won't even discuss his past, telling Gary that "it no longer has any relevance. It's excess baggage."[135]

Anatole attempts to permanently detatch his identity from his personal history by altering his language. As he says, "I try to speak in complete sentences ... It's a way of escaping the smelly undisciplined past with all its ridiculous customs and all its craziness - centuries of middle European anxiety."[136] Anatole plans to unjew himself by taking "out the urbanisms ... the question marks ... all that folk wisdom ... the inverted sentences." He plans to "use a completely different set of words and phrases" that will help him establish a new, healthy identity away from reductive traditions.[137]

Many other Logos players use language creatively to offset accepted norms. Raymond Toon uses the language of the sports broadcaster to escape the pressure of living up to the masculine code of the gridiron. When there are no sports to be called, he comforts himself by repeating complicated economic terms that he doesn't understand completely, but which he hopes will somehow connect him with the larger truths of the universe. As he says to himself in the cafeteria, "Redundant asset method. Capital Budgeting. Consolidation. Tax Anticipation Notes. Assessed value. Imputed Market Prices. Munitions. Maximized comparative risk."[138] Even though he doesn't understand the terminology, the words are comforting because they exist outside the language of the gridiron masculinity that Toon cannot handle.

Another player, Champ Conway, uses scientific language to probe the universe; he becomes fascinated with the frailties of humans, but also with the origins of life. Comparing humans to insects, he says that "In case of all out something-or-other, they'll probably take over the planet ... The insect resists fallout. He won't have birds feeding off him."[139] Undermining the coaches' notion that man's toughness will allow him to survive and find comfort in violence and conquest, Conway continues to say that "Insects are highly resistant to radioactivity. Man dies if he is exposed to six hundred units. Mr. insect can survive one hundred thousand units or more."[140] Conway is obsessed with insects and microbes, hoping they will reveal the secrets of life to him.

Billy Mast refuses to be content with the English language in any form and takes a course in the "untellable," in which the students search for new words and ideas by which they might be able to live better. Most of the words investigated are German because "if any words exist beyond speech, they are probably German."[141] While Mast doesn't understand German, he still finds the words comforting because they are new and therefore don't reinforce reductive masculine codes of behavior for him. After the Centrex game, Mast heals himself by repeating "a few German words" which "give him comfort" even though he is not sure what they all mean.[142] Direct meaning is unnecessary when the point is to glimpse something of the divine.

Scholar Thomas LeClair writes that "without stable identities as sources of actual communication, the characters often seem, like one character's favorite cliche, 'commissioned', as it were, by language itself."[143] Of course, Gary is the player who most freely utilizes language as a mechanism by which to understand and cope with the "militarization" process which he feels he is undergoing. Gary is, in fact, absolutely obsessed by language. He hates silence, saying that "of all the aspects of exile, silence pleased me the least."[144] Words such as "militarize" and phrases like "Suck in that gut and go harder" command his constant cerebral attention. He likes Anatole because he can compare him to an "overwritten paragraph," and meditates on nuclear war, in part, because he is riveted by "phrases like thermal hurricane, overkill ... kill-ratio [and] spasm war."[145]

Gary uses language in several ways, but his primary purpose is to escape the masculine identity in which he is ensnared. Gary admits that "I'm a chronic ball-breaker. I bull-shit myself."[146] Indeed, Gary is constantly creating ephemeral, alternate realities in order to fool his teammates and give himself momentary relief from his actual reality. When speedy running back, Taft Robinson, comes to Logos, Gary tells lineman Jerry Fallon that Robinson is actually a guard who will be taking Fallon's position: "Two hundred and fifty-five pounds of solid mahogany. They're thinking of playing him at guard. Left guard's your spot, isn't it? I just realized. Solid bronze right from the foundry. Coach calls him the fastest two-five-five in the country."[147] Even during the tense game with Centrex Gary manages to trick Roy Yellin, who is about to go into the game: "He'll kill you. He killed Cecil, didn't he? He'll drive you right back into the bench ... seventy-seven is going to eat your face. You'd better fake an injury. It's your only hope. If you try to play against that horrible thing, he'll send you home in pieces. He did it to Cecil and he'll do it to you."[148] Gary finally tells the frantic Yellin that he is "only kidding," admitting that "it helps me relax."[149]

For Gary, a byproduct of language experimentation is the subversion of traditions or societal norms. A brooding intellectual, he certainly overturns the reader's expectation of what a football player is like. He isn't concerned about winning, "has serious lapses," smokes pot before a game, and loses focus on the field "in order to make minor discoveries that have no bearing on anything."[150] He doesn't win the big game, and he doesn't get the pretty cheerleader for a girlfriend. Instead, he falls for an obese science-fiction junkie, Myna, because she "posits herself as the knowable word," and because she is "anti-historical," electing to be fat because she doesn't want to deal with the traditionally female responsibility of being beautiful.[151] Gary makes love to Myna in the library, instead of the more traditional bedroom. He plays war games with Major Staley in a hotel room instead of a classroom, and he refuses to take part in the traditional pre-game football preparations. In short, Gary does anything linguistically possible to upset traditional expectations in his attempt to move beyond the sanctioned patterns of masculinity that trap him and the dominant traditions and language which keep those patterns in place.

Of course, the boys' parents and coaches use language to try to convince the young men that they are, in fact, pointing them to something grand, something beyond themselves that will entrench them in a solid foundation of meaning. Gary's obsession with the game is due, in part, to his father's insistence that Gary play because he believes in the game as a character-builder. Further, he desperately wants to see his son succeed where he failed. As Gary says, "He had ambitions on my behalf and more or less at my expense. This is the custom among men who have failed to be heroes; their sons must prove that the seed was not impoverished."[152] In order to make sure Gary plays football, his father consistently bombards him with cliches meant to show how football can make a man into a winner. His father tells him to "Get cracking. Straighten out. Hang in. When the going gets tough, the tough get going. Suck in that gut and go harder. Backbone, will, mental toughness, desire— these were his themes."[153] For Gary, this patriarchal legacy, reinforced by his father's language, are too much for him to resist: "He put me in a football uniform early. Eventually, I received twenty-eight offers of athletic scholarship."[154]

More closely related to the players' reliance on football's asceticism are the dictates of head coach, Emmitt Creed, the man who, as his name indicates, wields power by controlling the spoken word at Logos College. Gary refers to him as the "avenging Patriarch," the man who convinces the players that he will teach them the secrets of living the simple life. Remaining distant from and "transparent" to the players, Creed seldom speaks. But when he does give the word, the players listen with reverence and awe. Tim Flanders affirms that "coach is a man of destiny."[155] During the Centrex rout, Jeff Elliot insists that "this team can come back. I believe in coach. He'll tell us what to do."[156] He builds separate, isolated living quarters and practice facilities for the football team, and isolates himself in a tower above them. He has them alone, and because of his distant nature and mysterious reputation, his words convince them that football "is only a game, but it's the only game" that will allow them to lead "the simple life."[157] Like an apocalyptic prophet, he sells them on the simplicity of violence: "Football is only brutal from a distance. In the middle of it, there's a calm, a tranquility. The players accept pain. There's a sense of order at the end of a running play with bodies strewn everywhere ... There's a harmony."[158] Creed's words convince the players of his ability to lead them to the secrets of life that can be learned through pain, sacrifice, and violence.

To convert their charges, Creed and the other Logos coaches rely on the power of tradition and language. Scholar Marc Osteen writes that "their discourse is authoritative ... because it ... demands 'unconditional allegiance.' It is fused with authority; it is a monologue— univocal, direct: it is the logos, the word of God."[159] Indeed, the coaches build the players up for the Centrex game by appealing to their deepest masculine fears of being dominated, of having their perfect season ruined and their lives upset: "They have definite sadistic tendencies. Centrex is mean. They're practically evil. And you better play mean ... They like to humiliate people ... They'll stomp blue shit out of you."[160] Coach Veech conditions the players to flail their bodies violently against each other, not disregarding but embracing the pain: "I want you to bust ass out there today. Hit those people ... until they look like sick little puppy dogs squatting down to crap."[161] When they make a mistake, he taunts them, asking "What are you feebs doing out there? ... You people are a bunch of feebs."[162] Another assistant, Coach Hauptfuhrer, screams at the players to "infringe. Infringe on them. Rape that man. Rape him. Ray-yape that man."[163] Coach Tweego appeals to the manhood of his charges, saying, "You're not firing out. That man is raping you. He's moving you at will. Sting him. Sting him. Sting him."[164]

Using a different strategy, Coach Clark attempts to mechanize the players with cold, technological language that seeks to order the ferocity of the violence: "What we want to do is establish a planning procedures approach whereby we neutralize the defense ... We use the aerial game to implement the ground game whereby we force their defense to respect the run ... It all depends on what eventuates."[165] Despite Clark's scholarly tone and sophisticated word choice, his aim is still the same: to militarize the players; to get them to believe that football's violence, pain, conquest, and denial will lead them to a better, more orderly existence. Of course most of the players eventually do subscribe to the philosophy of their fathers and coaches, completely dedicating themselves to the game. As Gary says, "A passion for simplicity, for the old true things ... filled our days and nights that summer."[166] Many, like Gary, actually feel secure and comforted by the violence of the game: "Hit and get hit; run over people. What a pretty sight. When coach says hit, we hit. It's so simple."[167] Gary even goes as far as to credit physical violence with giving him a spiritual connection with the universe, saying that "the universe was born in violence. Stars die violently. Elements are created out of violence ... I'm feeling very happy. Listen to these noises. Pop, pop, pop. Ving, ving. Existence without anxiety. Happiness."[168] They all buy in. As Gary says, "We were a lean, dedicated squad run by a hungry coach and his seven oppressive assistants. Some of us were ... simple; a few might be called outcasts; three or four, as on every football team, were crazy. But we were all ... dedicated."[169]

Of course, these attempts fail miserably and the players wind up bruised and battered physically and psychologically. The physical damage suffered by the players is evident at every practice and game, where painful injuries are so prevalent that they go largely unnoticed. Broken legs and arms are met with only casual interest. When Gary hurts his ribs against Centrex, the coaches rush him back into the fray, assuring him that "you're okay, you're okay, you're okay."[170] Ribs and collar bones are broken, ankles are twisted, players dehydrate and suffer countless cuts and bruises, but the coaches condition them to embrace the pain. Gary describes how, even at the first practice, the players learn to accept the effects of their football battles: "Deering ... got hit first by linebacker, Dennis Smee, who drove him into the ground, getting some belated and very nasty help from a tackle and another linebacker. Deering didn't move."[171] At this point, the reader expects a trainer to rush onto the field, but no medical help is forthcoming. "Two assistant coaches started shouting at him, telling him that he was defacing the landscape. The rest of us walked over and ran the next play. It all ended with two laps around the goalposts. Lloyd Philpot, Jr., a defensive end, fell down ... We left him there on his stomach, one leg twitching."[172]

After the Centrex game, the entire team is injured. Lenny Wells has a fractured arm; Conway has a broken collarbone; Lee Roy Tyler and Randy King have knee injuries. Of King, Billy Mast says, "They blind-sided him. Last play of the game. They caved it in on him."[173] Roy Yellin's ankle is "badly swollen ... purplish in color."[174] Dickie Kid has a separated shoulder; John Jessup bit his tongue; Jerry Fallon had his middle finger broken; "Bobby Iselin, pulled hamstring. Terry Madden, broken nose. Ron Steeples, mild concussion. Len Skink, worms. Everybody else, assorted contusions and lacerations."[175] When Myna Corbett asks Gary if he is all right, he replies, "They killed me."[176]

While the physical deterioration these players suffer through the course of the season is noteworthy, the psychological trauma is worse. The most obvious indication of this is the players' horrible fascination with violence and death. That violence is at the core of the identity of the players in *End Zone* is evident in the fact that every player is held hostage by violent, murderous, often morbid visions of mass destruction, nuclear war, genocide, and disturbing sexual fantasies. Gary Harkness, the novel's troubled anti-hero, admits that he is obsessed with nuclear disaster: "I liked reading about the deaths of tens of millions of people. I liked dwelling on the destruction of great cities ... Pleasure in the contemplation of millions dying and dead."[177] Gary's journeys into the desert are characterized by violent hallucinations: "I continued to look forward to each new puddle of destruction. Six megatons for Cairo. Typhoid and cholera for the Hudson River Valley ... Pleasure nourished itself on ... revulsion and dread. To complete the day I had to think of Milwaukee in flames."[178]

What is most fascinating about Gary's visions is the fact that, like many of the players, he relishes them. As he says of his sexual fantasies, "Closing my eyes, I wanted to dream that I put my hand between [a] dead girl's legs. Arousals of guilt had considerable appeal to me. I liked to be in bed, viewing after-images of morbid sex."[179] Likewise, Gary's roommate, Anatole Bloomberg, is actually invigorated through his violent visions because "life, happiness, fulfillment come surging out of particular forms of destructiveness. The moral system is enriched by violence."[180]

However, while each player has his own particular type of violent meditations, not all of the players willingly embrace them. Taft Robinson, for example, feels compelled to read about the historical murders of children even though it disgusts him: "I read about atrocities. I can't help it. I like to read about ovens, the showers, the experiments ... I like kids the best. Putting the torch to kids and their mamas. Smashing kids in the teeth with your rifle butt. Firing into ditches full of kids. That's my special interest. It's the worst thing there is. I can't bear it ... I don't know why I keep reading about it."[181]

Clearly, these players, who are strangely dependent on violence, long for a type of apocalyptic order and simplicity; this is an ascetic kind of longing that Marc Osteen describes as a need for a "violent cleansing."[182] They want an end to a life devoid of meaning; they want to blast away complexity and find whatever stability might be hidden in the rubble. To that end, the players routinely settle conflicts with acts of wild brutishness, the legitimacy of which is unquestioned. When Gary argues with huge linebacker, Moody Kimborough, over whether Robinson can wear sunglasses in the cafeteria, he expects to be punched: "I watched him coming toward the table ... Then I got up and hit him in the stomach ... He ... hit me in roughly the same spot. I sat down and tried to breathe."[183] No one bothers to stop the fight or even look to see who gets punched. Neither player thinks of trying to settle their dispute with words. Words, as Gary discovers, are "sinister" in that they can "lose their meanings."[184]Violence is both expected and accepted when there is an argument to be settled. This is the peculiar type of order that the players collectively recognize as being normal, even advantageous in their quest.

Even the coaching staff views physical combat and aggression as the panacea for whatever ails the players. After a poor practice for the upcoming showdown with Centrex, they encourage the players to get "rededicated" by having a blowout party, the intent of which is to rekindle the spirit of violence and competition that the coaches feel they need to be both successful and content. Gary describes the ensuing scene: "Creed suggested we have a beer party. There was a pissing contest with about twenty entries trying for altitude. The floor was covered with beer, urine and ketchup, and we were slipping and falling ... Clothes were torn and there was blood."[185] It's hard to picture a more desperate scene:

> There were tag-team wrestling matches, push-up contests, mock bull-fights and other events. Seven people were in a circle spitting on each other's shoes. Link Brownlee chugged a bottle of ketchup. Jim Deering and his brother traded punches to the mid-section, reviving a boyhood tradition. They took off Billy Mast's clothes and threw him through the front door. It was a horrible night.[186]

More than anything, the "games" of the party reveal how the players rely on games as structural forms which provide regulation and order to the violence with which they are so obsessed. Indeed, they seem to live for games, football or otherwise, that either give them a chance to celebrate their prowess against each other in combative contests, or which allow them to experiment with violence as a means by which to attain order and simplicity in their lives. The players even invent games, such as "Bang, You're Dead," for this very purpose. In this game the players attempt to shoot each other with their fingers, the point being to revel in one's ability to "kill" another person. As Gary says, "It has gradations, dark joys, a resonance. I started to kill selectively. To kill with impunity. To die in the celebration of ancient ways."[187] The act of dying is also highly valued by the players, whose mock exits to this world are replete with elaborate, grandiose gestures. They fall down steps, hang over rails, scream incoherently and double over in pain, enjoying the release of life and the simplicity of dying. Gary recounts, "I died well ... One afternoon, shot from behind, I staggered to the steps of the library. It was very relaxing ... it seemed absurd to get up."[188]

After the season is over, the players play a pick-up football game in the most brutal weather possible. There are no coaches, no trophies, or conference championships. They simply play for the enjoyment of regulating violence, of measuring themselves in combat, of probing the depths of violence to see what lies beneath. The game starts out as a passing game of two-hand touch. Gradually, however, the players make rules that reduce their options by eliminating complex variables such as passing or end runs. They regulate their playing space by restricting the plays to simple dives into the line and decide that the players must tackle with no gloves or coats in the bitter weather, allowing them to get as close to the primal violence of the game as possible:

> Jessup said gloves were outlawed. We were totally alone ... adrift within time and space. Jessup outlawed the placing of hands under armpits between plays. Then he outlawed huddles. Each play, he decreed, would be announced by the team with the ball." The players embrace the elements. "We were getting extremely basic, moving into elemental realms. Jessup outlawed passing plays; the hitting increased. Jessup banned end runs ... The snowfall was very heavy, limiting our vision to fifteen yards. It became a straight ahead game ... only the ball carrier could attempt to use evasion of finesse to avoid primal impact. Private battles continued until one man ... was buried in the snow. These individual contests raged in every play, each man grunting and panting, trying to overwhelm the other man. The cold was painful; it hurt.[189]

As Gary indicates, the players "find merit in the regulation," and relish the violent, primitive nature of the game in which they find a sense of peace, stability, order, and self-definition. Gary even admits that they "were comforted by the noise and the brunt of our bodies in contact, by the simple, physical warmth generated through violent action."[190] They will do anything to sift beneath the veneer of meaning to find the Truth that they hope lies underneath. Of course, they fail.

DeLillo makes it clear that their failure lies not just in the fact, pointed out so many times by other writers, that the football hero is socially constructed and that his extremely volatile identity is dependent on a number of changing variables. Instead, DeLillo asserts that they fail, that Creed fails, because human language is itself limited by material boundaries. The Word, the Logos, God may be out there and it may have the healing power of stability and permanence, but it is not reachable via the road of human language; it lies always just out of reach, leaving its pursuers frustrated and longing for resolution. In the case of these young men, the failure of their fathers' and coaches' language and traditions leads to a descent into a postmodern wasteland where they are left psychologically and spiritually unbalanced.

Scholar John Kucich explains that the players' dilemma centers around the fact that the language and traditions that effect them are in fact vestiges of the political, social, and economic realities of their forefathers:

> The real problem with DeLillo's male characters is that their attempts to oppose the power of mainstream American culture always involve the appropriation of gestures or poses that they cannot legitimately claim as their own—patterns of behavior, rather than principles or doctrines, that are conventionally rooted in someone else's social identity. And in this agony of social distance lies their impotence."[191]

Critic John Johnston reminds us that "In *End Zone* time is marked by the sudden and aleatory intrusion of death and silence on body and word ... events that seem to menace and disrupt the mind-body relationships."[192] Accordingly, Anatole continually taps his hands against any wall he can find, admitting that he's "an anguished physicist." His linguistic attempts to transcend history fail and he admits, "We are about to discover that austerity is our true mode. In our future meditations we may decide to seek the devil's death. In our silence and terror we may ... maim or kill whatever dark presence envelopes the world."[193] Clearly unbalanced, Bloomberg's final ruminations in the novel revolve around his fascination with contractions; an odd fascination with language is his focus until the very end. Even Gary admits that "we thought Bloomberg was crazy."[194]

Toon loses all control of his faculties during the Centrex game. Gary overhears him on the bench: "Capacity crowd. Emmett Big Bend Creed. Mike Mallon, they call him mad dog. Telcon. All color and excitement ... Woof. Three Rivers Stadium in Pittsburgh or Cincinnati ... And now back to our studios." His words simply serve as powerless gestures by which he tries to transcend and cope with the pressure of punishing the opposition and winning games under extreme conditions. Interestingly, his language completely fails in the football environment. As the Centrex game progresses, he nearly goes crazy:

> There they go. Chudko, now in for Butler ... Chudko, Chudko, majoring in airport commissary management ... College football ... there goes five, six, seven ... yards here at the Orange Bowl in sun-drenched Miami ... Capacity crowd. Emmett Big Bend Creed. Mike Mallon, they call him Mad Dog. Telcon ... Woof. Three Rivers Stadium in Pittsburgh or Cincinnati ... I'm sure glad I'm up here. D.C. Stadium in the heart of the nation's capital. Emmett Big Bend Creed. And there's more on tap next week when the Chicago Bears take on the ... Green Bay Packers of coach something something.[195]

Gary tells him "take it easy, ... try to get a grip on things."[196] But none of the players can use language to get the grip they truly desire.

Not only does the players' language lose meaning on the football field, regressing to "groans and barks," it also becomes wildly violent and childish. John Jessup taunts an opposing player, saying "You're a nipple-prick, an eensie weensie. You got a dong from a cereal box. Eensie, eensie, eensie."[197] Jessup threatens another player, "I get that sixty-two. I get that shit-piss and beat his black ass into the ground." When reminded that the man he is deriding is white, he says, "I know. They're all white ... those black fucks."[198] When Jessup throws an elbow into an opponent's face, yelling "Suckmouth. Peachpit. Shitfinger," the result is a bench clearing brawl in which several of his teammates are seriously injured. Sensible speech, orderly, comforting, controlled language is not possible on DeLillo's gridiron, despite the promises of the coaches that the players will find order there.

Bobby Luke is inserted in the novel as an example of what happens to players who are completely dedicated to Creed. Bobby "was famous for saying that he would go through a brick wall for Creed. Bobby was famous for it because he would say almost nothing else."[199] Gary postulates that Bobby is so firmly entrenched in the patriarchal tradition of being loyal to one's king or leader (in this case, the coach) that "it was a remark demanded by history."[200] As Gary comments:

> Bobby had this loyalty to give, this eager violence of the heart, and he would smash his body to manifest it. Tradition, of course, supported his sense of what was right. The words were old and true, full of reassurance, comfort and consolation. Men followed such words to their death because other men before them had done the same, and perhaps it was easier to die than to admit that the words could lose their meaning.[201]

However, it is evident from Bobby's language that his fierce adherence to his coach and to a masculine code based on violence and otherness (at least the conquest of other), has rendered him incapable of any expression other than that which forcefully objectifies his subject. The only three words the reader actually hears him snarl are "snatch," "gash," and "pussy," referring to the women who walk by while he is talking with Gary. His adherence to Creed has not only deprived him of meaningful language, but has also limited his personality and vocabulary to the reductive, violent word pool which allows Creed to control the players.

Other players fare no better. Conway is ignored and avoided because of his obsession with insects and the death of humankind. The language of science gets him nowhere. Billy Mast admits that he doesn't actually learn much in his course on the Untellable, and the economic terms that he and some other players use bring very little solace. Foreign languages fail, as does the language of social science.

In the end, Gary fails, too. He tries to resist anything that mainstream society accepts as normal. He tries to resist the lure of football. He plays incessantly with language as if he hopes that if he can just reconfigure the words he can find some way out of his suffocating condition.[202] As mentioned, he even smokes marijuana before a game to see if that will transport him to some new insight; he winds up walking off the field during the first series of downs. He has some hope that this will cause him to be thrown off the team, but Creed decides to make him captain instead, drawing him further into the apparatus. In the end, Gary realizes that "sport is an illusion ... the illusion that order is possible."[203] Finally, he collapses and has to be rushed to the hospital.

In all, DeLillo appears to offer only one linguistic alternative for his young men, embodied in Taft Robinson. Robinson, the only black player on the team, is fully objectified from the beginning of the novel. As Gary says, "they got him for his speed."[204] In order to escape a system which uses him, Robinson simply quits football, exclaiming that "I'm all through with football. I'm after smaller things. Less of white father watching me run."[205] He decides to abandon Creed's search for the simple life, confessing that "we taught each other nothing."[206]

Robinson's strategy in forming a new, fully subjective identity, relies on his ability to isolate himself in his room and "concentrate on my studies." His goal is to limit his living space to a definable area (another of DeLillo's extreme places) in which he controls the language and philosophy. Accordingly, he seeks to eliminate from his room all elements which remind him of the history and traditions that alienate him from himself, leaving all of the space empty except for a few specific items. He has two clocks because they "correct each other" and give the room "balance." As he tells Gary, "I've got this room fixed up just the way I want it. It's a well proportioned room. It has just the right number of objects. Everything is exactly where it should be."[207]

Most of all, Robinson tries to forge a new identity by controlling the language that circulates in his room. He has a radio, but listens "only at certain times of the day for certain periods of time. When time's up, I bring it into silence." He completely controls the language in his room, sometimes going "whole days without saying a word." Language becomes "a spiritual exercise. Silence, words, silence, silence."[208] He keeps an old marmalade jar only because he likes the words on it, saying with finality that "a new way of life requires a new language."[209] Yet, the reader can see that Taft is unstable and on the verge of a breakdown. DeLillo even reminds us of his fascination with child-killings, and though Taft declares triumphantly, "I'm through with football. I feel better every day,"[210] the reader is skeptical about the viability of his Invisible Man like strategy. Perhaps critic Francoise Hoppe sums it up best: "End

Zone may be read as the failure of … voices trying to assert their authority."[211] In the end, it appears that Robinson's linguistic attempts to find order and the Word will be just as impotent as those of the other players.

The ramifications of all of this failure are immense. Not only will the football hero fail as a positive, workable center for male identity, but every man-made, socially-constructed center will have the same problems. Every center will be bound by temporal conditions which change and inevitably devalue the center, and each template will be inscribed by language which is materially bound and can never quite reach the ultimate Word. Consider one of America's most unique masculine centers, the rugged individualist, the man who defines himself by independently making his own way in the world, often by taming his environment and establishing his own moral code outside of most institutional constructs. We have seen him in many forms from Natty Bumppo in Cooper's *Leatherstocking Tales*, to stories about real-life icons like Davy Crockett and Daniel Boone in the nineteenth century, to Tarzan in Edgar Rice Burrough's novels of the early twentieth century. The rugged individualist has been kept alive in westerns starring John Wayne and Clint Eastwood, among others. However, while it continues to be reconstructed for public consumption, it is not hard to see why it is not a workable center for men. All of its portrayals are impossibly romantic. Even if one concedes that the nineteenth century frontier was a simpler place than contemporary America, one would have to admit that not many men, if any, could go it alone for very long. Perhaps that's why we get only limited glimpses of Crockett or Boone. Their adventurous life could not be sustained for long, and as for Clint and the Duke, well, how many bullets can really come out of a six-shooter anyway? In the present day, we may lionize the image of the rugged individualist, but it is mostly our wishful projection of something we can't have. In reality, the rugged individualist always runs into countless societal structures, natural impediments, and loneliness.

How about the war hero? American men have a long history of romantic images regarding battle as a proving ground, a place to show that one has courage;

the ability to defend his family, values, and country; and the will to take human life. Like almost all heroes, the war hero has usually been cast as a community man, one who embodies and defends the values and interests of his clan, region, or country. He is the patriot, willing to sacrifice his life to make America great or advance the cause of freedom in the world. There are many such portrayals in American literary history, but there are also several depictions that undermine the war hero. Stephen Crane's *The Red Badge of Courage* features a protagonist who finds out that, contrary to the message sent by the bands, uniforms, polished rifles, and waving flags at recruiting stations, war is an ugly affair which snuffs out the lives of the young men trying to prove themselves. In Earnest Hemingway's *The Sun Also Rises*, Jake Barnes remains unfulfilled and depressed largely because he is impotent from his war wounds, leaving him with the capacity to love but not the physical ability. Ron Kovic's *Born on the Fourth of July* is an autobiographical novel that exposes how America's myth-making entices young, poor men to fight unjust wars for the benefit of rich men, wars that often leave them dead or seriously maimed. America's best writers have always understood the tragic limitations of the war hero as masculine center.

There are many types of heroic templates, but equally popular in recent times is the rebel, who is sometimes an anti-hero. The rebel is the classic negative center and has great appeal as well as a long tradition in a country founded by rebels. Think of Henry David Thoreau's "Essay on Civil Disobedience," which is still the intellectual foundation for so much of the protest that takes place in the United States. More appealing than Thoreau to the popular imagination have been outlaws like Billy the Kid, Jesse James, John Dillinger, and Bonnie and Clyde, who continue to be the subject of new films. The rebel thrives most in times of stifling conformity, which is why so many classic American anti-heroes hail from the 1950s. When asked what he was rebelling against in the 1951 film, *The Wild One*, Marlon Brando's character, Johnny, sneers, "What have you got?" James Dean became the quintessential rebel and hero to millions because of his role in *Rebel Without a Cause*, Elvis Presley gyrated into living rooms across the country, shaking his hips at musical convention, Ralph Ellison advocated a Camusian-like revolt in *Invisible Man,* and Jack Kerouac went *On The Road* in a bohemian search for spiritual enlightenment. They all rebelled and won admirers and even followers. Yet, these same authors, characters, and works undermine the credibility of the very center they extol. Johnny rebels, but ends up going nowhere with his life. James Dean did, in fact, live fast and die young, maintaining his heroic status. But he did have to die to do it; if he had grown much older, he could never have kept up the identity of the rebel. Ralph Ellison's protagonist cultivates anger and determination, but he winds up alone in a cellar with his chief form of rebellion being to steal electricity from the power company. He may be sticking it to the man, but he has no truly livable future. Even Kerouac's Sal Paradise finally understands that he has to get off the road and leave the bohemian search behind if he is actually to build a workable life; otherwise he might wind up like the true rebel of the book, Dean Moriarty, whose lifelong dedication to being a rebel clearly leads to his pathetic state at the end of the novel. The rebel has panache, but no staying power against age and the need to build a positive center that is constructive within the confines of established institutions.

What about the most universal of all masculine centers, power? The man of conquest has perhaps been the most compelling identity for which men have striven over the centuries. This is a center whose appeal is the acquisition of power, prestige, and privilege and is thus well-suited to capitalist democracy. It is maintained by continual conquest in any number of areas, including business or professional arenas; the pursuit of wealth; the use of political power; the conquest of women, nature, and foreign lands; and the exploitation of disempowered peoples. Captain Ahab was such a man in Herman Melville's *Moby Dick.* Of course, what he truly desired was meaning, but he tried to achieve it by conquering nature, by taming the seas and killing the great white whale. Another sterling example is Tom Buchanan, the racist bully of *The Great Gatsby.* He has enormous wealth, but it isn't enough. He can only be satisfied by humiliating those who would pretend to be his equal and demeaning those in the lower classes who might aspire for more. These two men, Ahab and

Buchanan, also represent the failings of this center. Its maintenance relies on continual conquest and thus makes everyone into a threatening enemy. It breeds isolation, anger, and paranoia, and as is the case with Ahab and Tom, often leads to the eventual destruction of the very person it is supposed to privilege. No wonder the richest, most powerful man in ancient history, King Solomon, cursed his wealth and power, recognizing that without a reliable grand narrative, all is vanity.

It would be easy enough to go on. All manmade centers follow this pattern. For instance, being a husband and father are certainly important roles for men, and novels such as Laura Ingalls Wilder's *Little House on the Prairie*, Rebecca Harding Davis' *Life in the Iron Mills*, Kate Chopin's *The Awakening*, Sloan Wilson's *The Man in the Gray Flannel Suit*, and Richard Ford's *Independence Day* all celebrate the power of the center of the family man. However, they also show how problematic it can be and how even this, perhaps the most noble of centers, is not in itself a sustainable grand narrative for men. Likewise, some men have relied on various traditions, often based on class or region of origin, to sustain themselves. However, books like Henry James' *The American*, William Faulkner's *The Sound and the Fury*, and Harold Frederick's *The Damnation of Theron Ware* critique the ability of the role of the gentleman, the Southern man of culture, and the religious man to function as stable narratives of meaning for men. As deeply entrenched in tradition as these centers might have been, times change and so do once time-honored customs, which come to be perceived as quaint at best and racist or sexist at worst. Another deeply rooted center is the renaissance man, which harks back at least to the period which bears its name, and is vividly described in early American works from Ben Franklin, Thomas Jefferson, and William Byrd. Yet, the emphasis for this center is being accomplished in a number of areas; one has to be nearly expert in music, art, business, language, athletics, technology, politics, religion, and any other area that is valued by society. Yet, one cannot be like Castiglione's courtier. It's just too hard, especially in a day of specialization, where one has to spend the better part of a lifetime becoming an expert in his specialty.

All of this is why other writers didn't offer an alternative center for men. In a material world with a language that can't approach the Divine, there are only other flimsy, faulty centers posing as the stable templates that men crave. Such centers will always fail as grand narratives.

So, what does one do? The deep desire for meaning that drives men never leaves and yet only material, false centers seem to present themselves as alternatives. DeLillo's characters show the reader what we usually do; we go back to the center most familiar or most attractive to us. That is why, ironically, these boys go back to football after it nearly kills them. Before he collapses, Gary always comes back to the game no matter how much it hurts him. As he says, "I discovered one simple truth. My life meant nothing without football."[212]

Like Gary, the other players are mystically drawn back to the game no matter how badly they are scarred mentally or physically. At the end of the Centrex game, the casualty list includes nearly everyone on the team. The players have not only endured an intense physical beating, but have also born the consistent verbal onslaught of the coaches, who loudly criticize their every move as they fall further behind Centrex. Still, the players long for the game and can't bear the thought of waiting until the next season. Gary says, "Without football, there was nothing, absolutely nothing, to do."[213] Billy Mast, a senior, is particularly distraught: "No more football. No more hitting. No more sweat and pain. No more fear. No more being ... cursed at by those insane coaches. No more getting kicked, elbowed or spat on. Literally spat on. It's awful. I can't accept it."[214] The seniors lament their graduation. It is as though they are addicted to the violent rhythms of the game, but in reality what they are addicted to is their quest for transcendent meaning, which they hope to find in familiar places such as the football field.

Thus, in the end they find that, though they must resist such false centers as the football hero, they must embrace them as well. For false centers are seemingly all that there are. This is ironic resistance: the recognizance that all possible centers in the material world, the world our language allows us to explore and negotiate, are socially constructed of ephemeral material, and that all will fail as the stable centers of meaning that they are simulating; and that, while we must resist their lure as stable centers around which to permanently base our identities, we must also embrace them; for they represent the options available in the world in which we live. DeLillo exposes this and seems to accept the gloomy conclusion that we will inevitably be incapacitated by this condition. Consider again Gary's final position in the novel. After insisting that "there must be something we can do," he collapses: "In the end they had to carry me to the infirmary and feed me through plastic tubes."[215] DeLillo has revealed to us the complex, elusive condition that traps us, ironic resistance, but leaves us with no way to negotiate its seemingly hopeless waters. Perhaps this is why some consider DeLillo to be the quintessential postmodern artist, willing to paint us into a corner of which Beckett would be proud. The question is, did he miss something?

Notes

[129] Don DeLillo, *End Zone* (Boston: Houghton-Mifflin, 1972) 22.

[130] DeLillo 237.

[131] DeLillo 10.

[132] DeLillo 134.

[133] DeLillo 77.

[134] DeLillo 77.

[135] DeLillo, 187.

[136] DeLillo 186.

[137] DeLillo 46.

[138] DeLillo 24.

[139] DeLillo 206.

[140] DeLillo 207.

[141] DeLillo 181.

[142] DeLillo 142.

[143] Thomas LeClair, "Deconstructing the Logos: Don DeLillo's *End Zone.*" *Modern Fiction Studies* 33 (Spring 1987) 107.

[144] DeLillo 30.

[145] DeLillo 21.

[146] DeLillo 26.

[147] DeLillo 9.

[148] DeLillo 127.

[149] DeLillo 127.

[150] DeLillo 234.

[151] DeLillo 218.

[152] DeLillo 17.

[153] DeLillo 16.

[154] DeLillo 18.

[155] DeLillo 57.

[156] DeLillo 122.

[157] DeLillo 15.

[158] DeLillo 199.

[159] Mark Osteen, "Against the End: Asceticism and Apocalypse in Don DeLillo's *End Zone*." *Papers on Language and Literature* 26 (Winter 1990) 148.

[160] DeLillo 95.

[161] DeLillo 161.

[162] DeLillo 137.

[163] DeLillo 130.

[164] DeLillo 120.

[165] DeLillo 28.

[166] DeLillo 4.

[167] DeLillo 35.

[168] DeLillo 121.

[169] DeLillo 4.

[170] DeLillo 135.

[171] DeLillo 11.

[172] DeLillo 11.

[173] DeLillo 146.

[174] DeLillo 147.

[175] DeLillo 147.

[176] DeLillo 149.

[177] DeLillo 20.

[178] DeLillo 43.

[179] DeLillo 73.

[180] DeLillo 215.

[181] DeLillo 240.

[182] Osteen 145.

[183] DeLillo 26.

[184] DeLillo 17.

[185] DeLillo 99.

[186] DeLillo 99.

[187] DeLillo 32.

[188] DeLillo 33.

[189] DeLillo 196.

[190] DeLillo 196.

[191] John Kucich, "Postmodern Politics: Don DeLillo and the Plight of the White Male Writer." *Michigan Quarterly Review* 27 (Spring 1988) 337.

[192] John Johnston, "Generic Difficulties in the Novels of Don DeLillo." *Critique: Studies in Modern Fiction* 30 (Summer 1989) 265.

[193] DeLillo 215.

[194] DeLillo 216.

[195] DeLillo 139.

[196] DeLillo 195.

[197] DeLillo 136.

[198] DeLillo 137.

[199] DeLillo 53.

[200] DeLillo 53.

[201] DeLillo 54.

[202] DeLillo 234.

[203] DeLillo 112.

[204] DeLillo 3.

[205] DeLillo 233.

[206] DeLillo 238.

[207] DeLillo 238.

[208] DeLillo 240.

[209] DeLillo 234.

[210] DeLillo 238.

[211] Francois Happe, "Voice and Authority in Don DeLillo's *End Zone.*" *French Review of American Studies* 54 (November 1992) 385.

[212] DeLillo 22.

[213] DeLillo 156.

[214] DeLillo 179.

[215] DeLillo 242.

Chapter 5
Managing Ironic Resistance: A Romantic Quest

The dilemma is clear. Manhood at its essence is stable meaning. None of the socially constructed alternatives continually being reworked around men are reliable; they are at best stop-gaps that delude us, staving off disaster for a few men for a short time. They are not healthy for most men most of the time, and thus, like so many of the characters in football novels and every other type of fiction, we want to resist them. Yet, we wind up embracing them as well because it seems like these alternatives are the only ones that exist. It's the ultimate postmodern dead-end. Is it any wonder so many men live desperate lives in which they move from one distraction to another?

Perhaps the fundamental problem is that, operating within the paradigms of Renaissance humanism, Enlightenment reason, and Modernist empiricism, we have for centuries sought to make meanings for manhood in the material realm with our minds and our own human languages. Yet, as philosophers from Plato to Jean Baudrillard, and writers from Henry Fielding to Don DeLillo have shown us, our finite, power-consumed minds and our flawed languages are incapable on their own of moving us beyond the self-referential, illusory centers that have been tried and retried for the last three hundred years.

Indeed, if we continue to follow these purely rationalist, material paradigms, we will likely continue to wallow in three readily available alternatives for coping with ironic resistance. The first is simply not to resist, which is what most men, consciously or (mostly) unconsciously, have always done. A man simply chooses or is chosen by a template, the athletic hero, the marine, the business mogul, the rebel, or any of many, many other roles. Perhaps he picks a role or combination of templates that is most valuable to him, to his larger culture, or to his more immediate sub-culture and simply goes with it. As evidenced in the analyses in the previous chapters, however, it seems as though whatever center or amalgamation of centers a man picks from the usual options is flawed, constantly subject to change as he and his society changes, and is likely not rooted in a larger narrative, a grand narrative if you will, that is anchored in something more stable than human words and concepts. Still, with a little luck, some men might see such a center or combination of centers guide them through life. As we have seen with the football hero, however, this usually doesn't happen. More often, men are jarred into reality by some changes or series of events that reveal the instability of the self-definition in question. Usually, it is difficult for the disillusioned man to recover, to find his footing and move on. He looks down to see that he has been standing on shifting sand and casts his glance about to see where the solid ground is. He can't find it anywhere and either panics or falls into a depressed, confused state in which he continues to live until he can attach himself to some other center. Often, the process only repeats itself. A good literary example of this is Philip Roth's *American Pastoral*, which chronicles the story of Seymour "Swede" Levov, a second generation American growing up in a tightly-knit, Jewish neighborhood in New Jersey. The reader follows Swede through his journey as an athletic hero, an all-American boy who plays his proscribed role without ever questioning its source or its viability. He is a credit to his family and his community, marries a pristine beauty queen, takes over the family business that his father worked so hard to build, and settles into his seemingly secure spot as a loving father and husband who has achieved the coveted American dream. Of course, that template, too, is subject to all the usual flaws, and Swede Levov's life gradually falls apart because his conception of himself will not allow him to adapt to changing conditions. His daughter is raped. She turns against him and his dream, commits terrorist acts in her town, killing their neighbors, and finally disappears. When Swede finally finds her, she blames him and his world view. Yet, Swede will not change. It's not that he doesn't want to. It's just that, like the boys in *End Zone* or Gavin Grey or countless other American heroes, he just doesn't know what to change to. Eventually, his wife leaves him, he has to give up his dream house, and he winds up a shadow of his former self, desperately trying to start over again on the only road he has ever known. Only now he is an older man and the reader is left feeling that, even though he is a good, sincere, moral man, he is to be pitied. He is not happy; he is not a success.[216] Roth is truly a writer of his generation and his protagonist, Swede Levov, would no doubt bear some resemblance to a fair number of modern men.

A second popular and decidedly much more audacious way to cope with ironic resistance is to circumvent it by admitting that there is no possibility of achieving a stable identity rooted in some powerful grand narrative anyway. This would more than likely be because there is, in the words of the famous postmodern philosopher Jacques Derrida, no transcendent signified, no God, no permanent ordering mechanism that stands outside of our material world, making sense of it, controlling it.[217] To others, like philosopher Richard Rorty, it could be because even if there were such a redoubtable super-force out there, it seems to many to be so remote and detached that we could never possibly hope to benefit from its alleged omniscience.[218] Either option precludes the establishment and maintenance of any sort of stable self. This might be viewed as depressing by some, but those who embrace this line of thinking choose to view it as liberating. The fact that there is no after-life, no ultimate point to existence which might unify one's self-definition, paves the way to view the enjoyment of material existence as life's chief goal. To that end, one is free to play lustily in the playground of transposable identities offered by various cultures and subcultures. There is no identity; there are only identities that one adopts to fit various situations. One becomes what one wants to be based on ability, one's needs, and most particularly, one's desires. It certainly looks like freedom, and many writers have explored the boundaries of such a tempting form of liberation. The verdict? It's not freedom. In fact, male characters adopting the postmodern strategy of free-play are usually depicted as following a similar pattern.

They start with feelings of excitement, not fulfillment, but anticipation because they can hop from one role to another, experiencing new challenges, places, and roles. Gradually, their experiences widen and it gets harder to find new sensations; the formerly intoxicating fluidity gets old. Ennui sets in. Even the pursuit of pleasure seems routine. In the end, they are left disillusioned and discontent. They sometimes wind up hopeless and the reason is clearly that, though they have made use of every usable identity to further their material accomplishments and pleasures, they wanted and needed something more: ultimate purpose and significance. Playing in the rubble of meaning for strictly earthly purposes just isn't enough.

There are many examples of this type of man in contemporary fiction, but one of my favorites is Carol Shields' depiction of Cuyler Goodwill in her Pulitzer Prize winning novel, *The Stone Diaries*. Cuyler is a classic liberal ironist. He moves seamlessly from one vocabulary to another, always refashioning himself in a way that pleases him, that makes him master of his circumstances. Cuyler admits later in life that his personal philosophy was always to master "one thing at a time."[219] It is true. As a young boy in Canada, he discovered his talent for carving. He developed it and became a professional. It was hard, grueling work, but he was driven to master it. He did and then he moved on to a new challenge fueled by a new need, sex. He desired his soon to be wife, Mercy, pursued her, married her, and reveled in her until she died during childbirth. Lost for a while, Cuyler began to search for answers as to why his wife was taken from him. He wanted God's answer and embarked on a spiritual quest, eventually coming to an understanding with God and erecting to Him an amazing monument that gained him national attention. Once he made peace with God, he was ready to tackle a new challenge and master it. His notoriety got him a job with the Indiana Limestone & Works Co., where he worked his way up to partner, perfecting his craft and his business skills. Over time, he gets bored with his role as business magnate and conquers the roles of community leader, public speaker, political official, and philanthropist. Finally, feeling as though he has mastered and grown tired of sex, religion, art, money, business, politics, and public opinion, he turns to the one thing he hasn't mastered: love. At age 60, he marries the beautiful 28 year old Maria, wins her love, and retires from public life. But even love, once won, will not sustain him in the role of devoted husband. Soon, "he feels he has lost his way in life," sees no point to his existence, and has no words to express his disillusionment.[220] Not only does he have no idea who he is after all of this mastering of various identities, he can't even remember the significance of Mercy's wedding ring, long his most prized possession, and why he had always wanted to give it to his only daughter, Daisy. One might suspect that, if Rorty were correct in surmising that the best way to negotiate a life without the possibility of a true center is to move fluidly from one discardable center to another, Cuyler would be happy and fulfilled at the end of his life. He is not. He is a shell of a man, wondering who he is and what life *means*.

And so, a third alternative emerges, the easiest and thus most popular of all. Simply put, it is distraction. Overwhelmed by the confusing array of masculine templates and images that come at them on a daily basis, many men opt to effectively ignore, or more exactly, distract themselves from the dilemma of manhood and identity. This quest for distraction has always existed, but has never been easier for men than it is now in America and the West. It is the familiar, well-chronicled story. Unbridled capitalism, controlled by powerful industrial and media interests, feeds off producing and selling distraction to all of us. No avenue is left unexplored and when one distraction falls from favor a new one is quickly produced. When it comes to manhood, the strategy is clear. Market the sensitive man, the masculinist, the feminist man, the rebel, the bad-boy, the family man, whatever you like. If it doesn't make money, refashion another template and sell, sell, sell. And so on, and so on. When men are fully bewildered, they will turn from the seemingly endless models of maleness to the endless forms of entertainment and sub-cultures manufactured for them.[221]

I know a man whose life, for nearly two years, essentially revolved around his dart leagues. Yes, there are dart leagues. Throwers usually "compete" twice a week, but you can be in more than one league if you'd like to spend more nights throwing darts. There are local, state, and national competitions. There are practices and there can be some significant traveling. One meets people, develops friendships, and spends a lot of time in and around dart league activities. It is your basic sub-culture. It occupied the attention of my friend for a while, and then he moved on—to motorcycles. Of course, there are hundreds upon hundreds of enjoyable distractions that are available to him if Sturgis loses its appeal. Video games are popular and men of all ages like to fight aliens, drive fast cars, or combat virtual bad guys. Televison shows offer temporary distraction. Reality shows draw quite a number of devotees, but if reality isn't your thing you can always try fantasy. Especially popular are fantasy sports leagues. Spectator sports continue to rivet millions of American men, allowing them to move seamlessly through a year as they follow the exploits of baseball and soccer in the summer, football in the fall, and hockey and basketball in the winter and spring. And, as my friends always remind me, never forget the power of auto racing and golf all year round. One of the more amusing books to blend the power of fantasy and fandom is Robert Coover's *The Universal Baseball Association of Henry J. Waugh*, but if you're a sports fan you had better be ready to laugh at your mania. I wasn't, but I quickly learned. It was either that or put the book down. Perhaps you are an athletic participant. I am. I use my hockey "B" leagues in a manner reminiscent of my friend's use of dart leagues. My father golfs four days a week and has in retirement become a professional golf club maker. Not into sports? How about photography, restoring antiques, painting, landscaping, music, building web-sites, electronics, cyber-chat, reading groups, traveling, collecting, trading stocks, cooking, flying, bird-watching, or learning a language. The sky is the limit. If we get bored, there's always our computer and what, disturbingly, seems to be the most popular distraction of all, pornography. The point is that there is plenty to keep our minds busy, little pockets of activity that offer temporal meaning. If one can string enough of them together enough of the time, one can evade fundamental questions of meaning for quite a while.

One of the best books to examine how distraction operates in men's lives is DeLillo's *White Noise*, which tells the desperate tale of Dr. Jack Gladney, a professor of Hitler Studies at College on the Hill. Jack is no anti-Semite. He is attracted to Hitler because of the dictator's ability to make people forget death, to be so focused on a man and his message, no matter how contorted, that they would march, as an entire nation, headlong into death as if it weren't even there. Jack fears death and he tries everything to distract himself from it. He marries different women, has several children, immerses himself in his discipline, and like many of the characters in the novel, dabbles in science, medicine, religion, and all of the many distractions offered by mass media. Interestingly, he is most comfortable in the mall or the supermarket, centers of consumerism where the act of buying things, of acquiring possessions, seems to be the magic elixir that will stave off death. However, even the shiny lights and bright colors don't really stop death, as Jack finds out when he is exposed to a deadly toxin. Death will eventually intrude upon and prevail over all of our distractions, demanding that we answer the deeper questions about meaning and significance that we have been avoiding. Jack never does find answers to these questions and his decision to try to re-embrace distraction at the end of the novel is unconvincing, a resigned gesture of a tired man. Distraction fails him, just as it fails the other characters in the novel, just as it failed with disastrous consequences the people of Nazi Germany, just as it fails men today.[222]

Clearly, the rational, purely material approaches we have relied upon to find meaning and purpose in our lives have not produced a foundation in which men can fashion stable, healthy identities. It seems that humans operating by themselves in a brutal world of toil and struggle over resources and power simply don't have it in them to produce such a self-conception. A foundation upon which to base an identity could only come from a source that is outside of us, outside of the material realm. For us to use or make sense of all of the fragile centers that we continually recycle we need a supernatural context in which to place them. In short, we need some romance to compliment our rationalism. This is hardly a new idea. Consider how many great men have been men of faith. Christians Dietrich Bonhoeffer,[223] who died at the hands of the Nazis because he was helping Jews escape Germany, William Wilberforce,[224] who fought for eighteen years in Parliament to get his bill that would outlaw slavery in England passed, and George Washington Carver,[225] who passed up cushy corporate jobs to use his inventive skills on behalf of poor farmers, were all driven by their love for Christ. Uriah Levy, an Orthodox Jew, was so motivated by his faith in God that he endured years of discrimination to rise to the rank of Commodore in the US Navy. Once he became a gatekeeper, he used his power to introduce anti-discrimination regulations into the navy; he abolished flogging and consistently worked to make sure young, poor seamen had good working conditions and fair pay. When the US Army built its first Jewish Temple, they dedicated it to Commodore Levy.[226] Dedicated Muslim men of faith have been living lives of service for hundreds of years, but some recent Muslim converts have been just as dedicated to human rights. Consider Yusuf Islam, formerly known as pop singer Cat Stevens, who gave up fame and fortune to pursue a quiet, contemplative life. Islam did not adopt the lifestyle of a recluse, however. He began to write religious music, making enough money to open Small Kindness, a non-profit organization dedicated to helping poor children, many of whom are victims of war, have a chance at a better life.[227] Perhaps the two most noteworthy crusaders for human rights in the twentieth century, Mohandas Ghandi, a Hindu, and the Dalai Lamas, the Buddhist leader who has lived in exile in India since the Chinese communists drove him from Tibet in 1959, have been men who sacrificed themselves for others in the name of their faiths. Of course, most of the men who have lived powerful lives of self-sacrifice in the name of others have been simple, unsuspecting men whose daily work has gone largely unnoticed. These are men like Virsing Rathod, a devout Hindu who risked his life one night in March of 2002 by dragging Muslims out of a burning building and hiding them in his house as angry mobs motivated by, of all things, religious hatred, stormed the streets in search of Muslims. Nearly 550 Muslims were killed, but the fact that Rathod saved several lives didn't impress him. "I did it out of humanity," he said, "because in my heart I knew it was the right thing to do."[228] Like all of these men, we must hope that a supernatural power, God (in my opinion) if you will, not only exists, but that this God has a plan, an overarching order, a grand narrative, in mind. Though we cannot fully decipher it, we have to believe it is there and that, though we are given free will to act, God is in control, can always exert ultimate authority over worldly affairs, and will in the end make our lives eternally meaningful by rewarding or punishing our actions after our deaths. Nothing seems so strange and irrational as faith in the unseen and unfathomable, but, as Soren Kierkegaard wrote in *Fear and Trembling* of Abraham, who was willing to sacrifice his own son, Isaac, because God told him to: "Abraham believed the preposterous ... He knew it was God the Almighty who was trying him. He knew it was the hardest sacrifice that could be required of him, but he knew also that no sacrifice was too hard when God required it, and he drew the knife."[229] Through his act of obedience, Abraham himself earns his eventual destiny as the seminal father of three world religions. For his faith is rewarded by God. He spares Isaac, who will go on to lead the nation of Israel. Kiekegaard understood the message perfectly: from faith in the unseen comes reliable meaning, purpose, and order. I agree with the great Danish philosopher. The best alternative, indeed the only affirming alternative for men, is the cultivation of faith, a surpassingly romantic act.

All of the men mentioned above have faith in common. They do not have the same faith, but they all have a type of faith that has some notable characteristics. First, faith hinges on the belief that there exists a higher reality beyond what is materially visible, a transcendent realm occupied by a controlling force, often called God, Allah, Brahma, or some other name. This redoubtable force is both signifier and signified, a guiding force who exists beyond language and who has a divine plan for the universe, a grand narrative of truth, that provides order to human existence. Second, that meta-narrative must, in part, be revealed to us. Usually, this revelation is part of a holy text, *The Holy Bible* for Christians, *The Talmud* for Jews, *The Koran* for Muslims, *The Book of Mormon* for The Church of Latter Day Saints, *The Vedas* or *The Upanishads* for Hindus, or the *Tripitaka* and the *Sutras* for Buddhists. Third, faith relies on the idea that, although human language and motives are imperfect, they are good enough to allow people to understand this revelation, at least in part. Fourth, faith must be sustainable via this understandable grand narrative in at least three ways. It must be true that the more one pursues the dictates of such a narrative, the more peaceful and joyous one becomes. This is not to say that one will be happy all of the time. Happiness and sadness come and go with the material fluctuations of life. Joy and peace simply refer to our ability to recognize that, as material conditions, happiness can be enjoyed without it becoming the benchmark for evaluating our success and sadness can be endured without despair. It's not anything remotely close to stoicism. It's just an eternal context that allows a person to make sense of life's beauty and pain. In addition, the more one pursues the narrative, the more one is able to make sense of all of the false, illusory narratives that surround us, trying to convince us that they are healthy and stable. For instance, one's faith does not negate the possibility of one enjoying being a football hero, a rock star, a father, a rebel, a reformer, or any of life's other roles and experiences. It does, however, allow one to avoid adopting any of those unstable roles as holistic identities. Instead, faith allows a man to take the best of any given role or experience and resituate it in a larger narrative rooted in supernatural stability. In this way, being a football hero only becomes part of who a man is, and he can weave his status as an athlete into the grand narrative that is actually fueling his self-conception. And speaking of that conception, a faith is most fundamentally sustaining in that the more a man believes in the narrative the more he should be able to forget himself in favor of God and other people and to place his identity and his hopes for success in two things: making the world a better place for others and redefining his own success in terms of eternal reward for his actions toward his fellow man. Selfless servanthood dedicated to a better life for others, a kinder world, and the possibility of eternal reward, is the end of faith, and ironically, the end and beginning of self.

Thus, this type of spiritual quest for faith, the quest for an identity rooted in a divine order, is the true essence of manhood and the only way out of the dilemma of ironic resistance. Some fine literature reveals this to be true. Many Jewish writers have addressed this topic, including such literary heavyweights as Roth, Isaac Singer, Bernard Malamud, Saul Bellow, and Elie Wiesel. One of the best is Chaim Potok, whose companion novels, *The Chosen* (1967) and *The Promise* (1970), chronicle the spiritual growth of two Jewish boys as they negotiate the complex waters of faith and adult responsibilities in a secular world. As powerful as these two works are, my favorite of Potok's novels is *The Book of Lights* (1981), in which we encounter Gershon Loran, an orphan who comes to live with his Orthodox Jewish grandparents in Brooklyn. Gershon's world is noticeably ugly. His neighborhood is full of dilapidated homes, unsavory characters, crime, garbage, soot, and arson fires. He somehow manages to survive and even flourish, proving that something beautiful can come from foul soil. He goes to a Jewish college and meets Arthur Leiden, an emotionally frail, but brilliant physics student who has left Harvard because he feels he is somehow being pushed along the same path as his father, a famous physicist who had helped perfect the atomic bombs that were dropped on Hiroshima and Nagasaki. Arthur is haunted by guilt and feels he is trapped by a "death light," presumably the massive glow of the atomic blasts that killed so many innocent people. Fortunately for Arthur, Gershon has been well-schooled in the dictates of the *Talmud*. At college Gershon bolsters his rational, logical approach to knowing God with his studies of the cabala, which focus on the *Zohar*, the great book of Jewish mysticism. Slowly, Gershon's faith grows and he thinks he may want to become a Rabbi. Arthur is encouraged by Gershon to seek a light greater than the death light that haunts him. As their friendship deepens, Arthur begins to feel some of the hope that Gershon is radiating. He does not commit suicide; he staves off madness, embraces hope, and makes it through school. Gershon wins an award named after Arthur's father, but decides to take some time to further study the *Zohar*. Eventually, he becomes a chaplain in the U.S. Army and faithfully serves troops in Korea. He wins their respect because he is selfless; he not only gives of himself for them, but he sacrifices his own needs and desires for the local villagers, who suffer in poverty and squalor. Armed with the intellectual power of the *Talmud* and the emotional inspiration of the *Zohar*, Gershon senses the beauty of God's love and understands that it is up to him to combat the ugliness that has always surrounded him by allowing God's light to shine on the world through his actions. In the final chapters of the novel, Gershon travels to Japan to meet Arthur, who is still desperately trying to combat the death light that blinds him. Gershon convinces him that he can put this death light, this false narrative that forces him into the role of a guilty killer, into the larger context of God's healing light. Arthur does it. In some mysterious fashion, he embraces this meta-narrative, travels to Hiroshima, prays openly for forgiveness and restoration, and seemingly finds it. Though he dies soon thereafter in a plane crash, the reader is left with the impression that he has made peace with his ghosts. The novel ends with Gershon putting Arthur's family at ease about his last hours and then flying to Jerusalem where he will study the sacred texts in hopes of absorbing more of God's mysterious, radiant light, so that he can go about his business of showing others how that light can bring beauty and meaning into the ugliness of a selfish world. In the end, he has joy.[230]

The same can be said for Samba Diallo, the protagonist of Cheikh Hamidou Kane's *Ambiguous Adventure* (1961), a novel in the rich tradition of Islamic literature that focuses on a man's quest for meaning and purpose. Samba is the son of a Muslim religious leader who grows up as a colonial subject in French Senegal. His first twenty years are characterized by intense religious education. Under a tough yet compassionate teacher, Thierno, Samba memorizes *The Koran* and internalizes its lessons. He fears Thierno, but he also admires him because of how he treats people with honor and dignity, and because of how he has dedicated his life to helping people get to know Allah by living sacrificially. Diallo, too, feels this spirit and the joy it brings. However, his spiritual health and happiness are not to last. As the future leader of his colonized people, he must learn western customs. The second half of the novel covers his education under French instructors both in Senegal and in Paris. The reader watches as Diallo learns to trust science and reason over religion, to appreciate atheism as the proper faith for the enlightened mind, and to accept material acquisition and social advancement as the chief aims of life. The further Diallo drifts from his pursuit of the grand narrative revealed to him in *The Koran*, the more he is susceptible to the limited roles offered to him as a colonial subject by his new western narrative. Naturally, what he has a hard time seeing without the teachings of his youth is that all of these roles are deceptive. He might, for instance, be allowed to dress and talk like a gentleman; he might even be allowed some upper-class perks such as a nice house, money, or a position in the government that carries with it a fancy title. But he will always be a colonial subject. He will never really be a gentleman or a leader or a reformer. He will only be allowed to play one or more of those roles in a story written by his oppressors. In effect, he is being bought off with a few trinkets so that he will unwittingly keep his people in "their place." Without the aid of the discredited meta-narrative of his youth to put this grand deception in context and thereby to thrust it into a light that will expose it for what it is, he degenerates into a shell of a man. The power of the narrative of faith that he learned as a happy, vigorous, purposeful young man is made more obvious by its absence. Finally, on the edge of despair, Dialla returns to his village when Thierno dies. He goes to his teacher's grave to pay his respects, hoping that somehow his faith will be revived. When he cannot pray, his silence is mistaken for an insult by a man known only as The Fool, an unstable man who is representative of the type of person for whom Thierno dedicated his life. Enraged, the crazed beggar stabs Diallo, dealing him a mortal blow. As Diallo slowly dies, he cries out to Allah and undergoes a mystical change. He suddenly feels connected with Allah, Thierno, his father, and the narrative that had given him such happiness and confidence as a young man. He remembers who he is and what the point to life is, to serve others and radiate the grace of the almighty. Having learned how to live, he dies in peace.[231]

Another character whose quest for faith ends with him learning how to live is Tayo, the resilient Laguna hero of Leslie Marmon Silko's novel, *Ceremony* (1977), one of the best of several Native-American works that deal with male identity. Tayo's

118

predicament is similar to Diallo's in that he is an object who is being forced to play destructive roles in a story written by those who see him only as a pawn to be sacrificed for their greater good. Like Diallo, Tayo and his friends find themselves in an environment in which they seem to enjoy the same identity their white counterparts do. During World War II, deep in Japanese jungles, and after the war in European cities whose war-ravaged citizens feel indebted to their American liberators, Tayo and his friends are soldiers. They have the same uniforms as the white men, they can kill alongside them, they can eat and drink with them, they are paid the same, and they can have sex with as many white women as will have them. They are soldiers, or so it would seem. As soon as the threat to the country has passed, the Indians are discharged and they are no longer soldiers. In fact, it becomes clear that they never were soldiers; they were just allowed to play soldier for a little while because it was to the advantage of the white nation in whose story they were acting. Back home on the reservation, their real status is clear. They are to be invisible, to stay on their reservation, and devoid of economic and educational opportunities, revert to the habits of all men bereft of hope: drinking, gambling, and fighting. Since they would certainly go to prison for assaulting whites, they are left to vent their frustrations on each other. This is their role in the white story, a role that allows whites to use their labor when it is needed and justify their relegation to the backwater of American society when they aren't needed on the charges that the Indians lack character, something which seemingly is consistently manifested by the drunkenness and other bad habits into which their hopelessness forces them. It is the classic case of othering and then blaming the victim. The problem is that it's easy for us to see how it works from a distance; it is nearly impossible for someone like Tayo to understand it when it is happening to him. He doesn't comprehend it, but he feels it, and he eventually collapses. Sadly, the white doctors think he is suffering from combat fatigue. Yet, his main symptom that the doctors cannot understand is that he feels like "white smoke."[232] What he means without knowing it is that the white story in which he is thrust has rendered him invisible; it is killing him and there is seemingly nothing he can do. However, in the last half of the novel, Tayo finds that there is recourse. With the aid of an old medicine man named Betonie, Tayo learns the ancient stories that emanated from the creator, Ts'its'tsi'nako, also known as Thought-Woman, and which sustained his people for centuries. These ancient texts have nearly been ridiculed out of existence. The Lagunas have been taught to hate their heritage. However, the more Tayo learns about this larger forgotten narrative the healthier he gets. He begins to understand who he is, why he is sick, and what he needs to do to get better. By the time he completes the ancient scalp ceremony, he has figured out how to put the smaller white narrative that has trapped him within the exposing light of Ts'its'tsi'nako's narrative. He is no longer trapped. At one with Thought-Woman and the sacred stories that make up his spiritual heritage, he now feels connected to the land, his people, and all other peoples as well. He knows his duty is to take care of his family and nature and to sacrifice his own well-being in order to show all people how paradigms of conquest and acquisition create inequalities that demean both the haves and the have nots. Once he has an identity rooted in a stable grand narrative, Tayo learns what Diallo, Samba, and Gershon Loran learned: that manhood is having a sense of meaning and purpose that allows a man to resist harmful narratives and sow toward the greater good by denying himself in favor of others and by loving and trying to help his oppressors even as he resists their oppression. Not surprisingly, Tayo is no longer sick at the end of the novel. He is no longer smoke. He will still have to deal with racism, but he has the means with which to confront it. He is vibrant and peaceful.[233]

It is interesting that literary works that feature a man's *successful* quest for meaning are different in that, while there is always a higher power at work with whose abiding narrative the protagonist must align himself, that power has diverse depictions. Eastern religions such as Hinduism and Buddhism, for instance, offer very different versions of a man's development of a healthy identity than their Western counterparts. There is a long history of works in the Hindu tradition that match this description. *The Abhijnansakuntalam, The Immortal Tales, King Vicram* and *The Ghost, Panchatantra, Krishnavatara,* and *Saints of Maharashtra* are all ancient Hindu texts that feature male quests. R. K. Narayan's *The Vendor of Sweets* (1967) and V.S. Naipaul's *Finding The Center* (1986) are two well-known modern novels that have continued this tradition. Yet, the Hindu influence has been felt in the United States as well, especially in the works of writers such as Ralph Waldo Emerson, whose famous poem, "Brahma," reveals that meanings for manhood can be fused within a sixteen line poem as well as a three-hundred page novel. Inspired by *The Vedas* and *The Upanishads,* Emerson urges his readers to see through the illusions offered by worldly society. Fame, money, desire, anger, happiness, sadness, victory, and defeat will all fade into nothingness, and questing after these things or even acting as the result of them will only prevent one from becoming whole, which is Emerson's goal. For it is not that the material world is useless or to be avoided. It's just that one needs to have the proper spiritual framework through which to view one's experiences, an overarching narrative that is rooted in the divine that allows one to make sense of life's complexities. One does this by becoming one with the Brahma, the great oneness of spirit that not only guides the universe, but actually is the universe. Emerson calls Brahma the Oversoul. A man unifies himself with it by studying the sacred texts, meditating on their teachings, and concentrating on doing good which, you guessed it, is understood as losing oneself in the service of others. Thus, though the Hindu quest is a bit different, the end result is familiar: to find oneself, lose oneself in the power of servanthood. For the speaker of the poem, this brings unity and peace.[234]

Another variation on this theme is found in Herman Hesse's *Siddhartha* (1922), a classic novel in the Buddhist tradition. The tale is the story of Siddhartha, the son of a Brahman, who is seeking enlightenment. He learns Buddhist wisdom at the feet of great scholars, but the knowledge does not yield peace. He then joins the Samanas, a sect of ascetics that practice an extreme and solitary form of self-denial. This, too, leaves him unfulfilled. Discouraged with Buddhism, he turns in full force to materialistic pursuits. He satisfies all of his appetites and becomes in the view of his society a grand success. However, he is more unhappy than ever before. In despair, he considers suicide. He walks into the woods one day and just keeps walking, leaving behind his worldly goods. He walks until he comes to a great river in the middle of the wilderness. Fatigued, he kneels on the banks of the river and begins to yield to the suicidal thoughts that haunt him. However, the longer he looks at and listens to the river, the longer he feels its rhythms, the more he feels another voice welling up inside him. From his childhood teachings, he recognizes it as the great "Om," the sacred sound that begins and ends all Buddhist prayers. Suddenly and surprisingly, and much like Gershon Loran, he is able to marry all of his spiritual knowledge with genuine feeling. The river proves to be his most important sacred text. For it at once contains and is the great spirit of the universe, and it allows him to make sense of Bhuddist teachings so that he can refashion the asceticism of the Samanas in a way that will move him from isolated self-denial to purposeful self-sacrifice for others. As he continues to learn and feel the unity of the universe, he experiences deeper enlightenment. The novel ends with him meeting his lifelong friend, Govinda, whose spiritual journey has lead him to confusion. Govinda asks Siddhartha for help, and Siddhartha asks his friend to kiss him. Govinda does and immediately experiences illumination. It is romantic, so much so that it seems too simplistic to modern readers. But the point is clear. Siddhartha's journey is complete. He has tapped into the Great Brahma of the universe and it has made his knowledge whole. It has given purpose and energy to the ideal of selfless service, and he has served Govinda with the greatest gift one could give: enlightenment. At the end of the novel, both men have found peace.[235]

In the final analysis, few traditions have a longer and richer literary history featuring men who have found reliable meaning and its accompanying peace than Christianity. Contemporary Christian artists writing about men's lives inherit a legacy that includes John Milton's *Paradise Lost* (1667), Dante Alighieri's *Divine Comedy* (1321), John Bunyan's *Pilgrim's Progress* (1678), Daniel Defoe's *Robinson Crusoe* (1719), Charles Dickens' *A Tale of Two Cities* (1859), Charlotte Bronte's

Jane Eyre (1850), G.K. Chesterton's *Orthodoxy* (1909), C.S. Lewis' *Till We Have Faces* (1956), the sermons of George Whitefield and Jonathon Edwards, and the poetry of such men as John Donne, George Herbert, T.S. Eliot, and Thomas Merton. Those names barely scratch the surface. All of these artists, and many more, proceed from the belief that there is a God who has revealed himself in *The Holy Bible*, that we can know, at least in part, God's directives, and that if we follow them we will be whole. A notable contemporary example of this faith put into practice is Walker Percy's novel, *The Second Coming* (1980), the touching tale of Will Barrett, a wealthy, successful lawyer who is haunted by his past and discouraged by his present life of numbing country club socials and phony relationships. He has tried the American Dream, complete with a funky brand of upper-class Episcopalianism, but it has brought him to a dead end. Then, as the result of a stray golf shot, he meets Allison, a young, poor, emotionally unstable girl who has just been released from a mental hospital. She is living in an abandoned greenhouse just off the golf course that Will plays nearly every day. She is quixotic and is as estranged from her family and peers as Will is from his. It seems an unlikely match, but Allison is able to give Will something he has never had, love. She sacrifices herself for him and inspires in him true faith. He, in turn, finds the courage to confront his past and learns how to negotiate his present. He loves her and will sacrifice his life for her and will also use his wealth and power to serve those who are hurting. This is exactly why Jesus Christ came, to sacrifice himself for others, and what he commanded his followers to do, to aid the poor, the weak and the helpless. Will Barrett comes to have faith that this is true, and he finally finds joy and possibility in life.[236]

It is fascinating to note that so many of the works that feature men finding an identity that produces contentment follow this pattern. Cutting across time, race, nationality, and most notably, religion, all of these pieces of art feature protagonists who quest for meaning and find it in a faith rooted in a grand narrative that meets all of the criteria listed earlier this chapter. They are especially united in the final product of their faith, the ability of their male protagonists to form identities which center

123

around sacrificing for others, which allow them to make sense of false identities that had trapped them, and which produce a sense of both material and eternal security within them. This is manhood.

Of course, it must be acknowledged that there are problems with this process. Faith in a grand narrative rooted in the divine necessarily means religion, and religion gone wrong can be one of the most dangerous false centers for men. In recent times, Islamic terrorists have garnered considerable media coverage. Osama Bin Laden and Muhammad Al-Zarquowi have been the most visible and most reviled Muslim extremists, and their quoting of the *Koran* after the September 11, 2001 bombing of the World Trade Center in New York City inextricably linked violence and Islam in the minds of many western observers. This connection is reinforced for Americans every evening on the nightly news where we watch Al-Queda, Hamas, the Islamic Salvation Front, The Taliban, and many other Islamic fundamentalist groups claim responsibility in the name of Allah for acts of violence against Israel, the United States, Great Britain, or any other country or group of people whose policies or actions they have deemed as the work of the infidels. Even as I was writing this chapter, CNN was broadcasting live coverage of a young Muslim named Mohammed Reza Taheri-azar who decided to drive his jeep into a populated area at the University of North Carolina at Chapel Hill with the intent to harm as many students as possible. His goal? To defend Islam and his homeland of Iran against western aggression symbolized by recent American military incursions into Iraq and the Middle East.[237] Unfortunately, media images of men like Mr. Taheri-azar have become all too commonplace.

Still, religious fanaticism is hardly limited to Muslims. Men of all faiths have consistently been driven by their convictions to commit heinous acts that in their minds are purely righteous. On February 25, 1994, Dr. Baruch Goldstein, a member of a radical Zionist group located in the isolated Kiryat Arba settlement on the West Bank, walked into the Tomb of Patriarchs in Hebron with a machine gun and murdered thirty Muslims while they were praying. To Goldstein, and other radical

Jewish activists like Meir Kahane and Yoel Lerner, violent acts like this are justified by the *Torah*. In the same way, Christian terrorists freely quote the *Holy Bible* even as they kill the innocent. Dating back to the crusades and beyond, there are many examples of the Christian Church engaging in acts of institutional terror for the sake of worldly power.

However, this book is about individual men and their identities, and there is no shortage of examples of Christian men whose version of faith inspired them to commit crimes in the name of God. The frightening Christian Identity Movement has given us Eric Rudolph, who among other buildings bombed abortion clinics in Birmingham, Alabama and Atlanta, Georgia, and lesbian bars around the Atlanta area, before setting off an explosion at the 1996 summer Olympics in Atlanta; Buford Furrow, who assaulted a Jewish Center in 1999 in Grenada Hills, California; and the notorious Timothy McVeigh, who destroyed the Oklahoma City federal building in 1995 with hundreds of innocent people still inside. Abortion and homosexuality particularly seem to inspire the wrath of Christian extremists. In 1984, Mike Bray, believing he was called by God to eradicate abortion from the face of the Earth, began a string of clinic bombings in Delaware, Virginia, and Maryland that eventually resulted in his 1989 conviction. Bray's friend, Paul Hill, picked up where he left off, killing Dr. John Britton and his escort outside of a Florida clinic in 1994. The list goes on and on.[238]

Though Islamic, Jewish, and Christian terrorists get the lion's share of the exposure, religion as a dangerous false center is hardly limited to Islam, Judaism, and Christianity. In India and Pakistan, Hindu violence against Muslims, Christians, and other religious minorities has resulted in thousands of casualties in the last few years alone. Hindu nationalists compose India's dominant political party, the Bharatiya Janata Party (BJP), and have routinely overlooked individual acts of Hindu violence toward minorities, especially the Sikhs. Of course, this has resulted in acts of revenge by the Sikhs, whose religion also calls for non-violence. One such incident occurred in 1995 when a group of Sikhs lead by religious zealot Simranjit Singh Mann bombed the secretariate building in the state capital of Chandighar, killing the chief minister of state and fifteen of his aides. Though not widely covered by the western media, Sikh-Hindu violence is a daily affair, much like the Arab-Israeli violence that dominates the Middle East. Even Buddhists, whose religious books and stories call more stridently for peace and goodwill as much or more than any other major world religion, have among their fold many people who pervert doctrine in the name of a warped masculine identity. Such was the case with members of the Aum Shinrikyo sect of Japanese Buddhism, some of whose members released vials of the poisonous sarin gas on a Tokyo subway in March of 1995. Several innocent people were killed and thousands were seriously injured. One of the ringleaders, Takeshi Nakamura, said that he was inspired by Master Sholo Asahara, who had advised him to become a great man, one whose karma would allow him to "survive and create a new and transcendent human world" once the present, sinful world of material acquisition has been destroyed.[239]

Taheri-azar, Goldstein, Brey, Rudolph, Furrow, Mann, Nakamura and many male religious terrorists all had something in common. They associated manhood with a spiritual quest that resulted in a warped sense of absolute certainty regarding what they saw as their violent, God-sanctioned duties. Mark Juergensmeyer, Director of Global and International Studies at the University of California, Santa Barbara, confirms that such men labor under one of the most powerful false centers in the history of humanity, the martyr, who seeks "the larger framework of order that religious language provides."[240] The men listed above were not "trying to avoid life but to fulfill it in what they considered to be an act of both personal and social redemption."[241]

So, there is danger in the spiritual quest for meaning, which can go awry and result in the construction of just another mirage masquerading as stable meaning. However, no part of the human experience is without danger, and in the end, it is still true that the spiritual quest is worth the risk for men. For it is the only way beyond ironic resistance, beyond the self.

The final question is, then, how do we quest? Perhaps the first thing to be clearly and emphatically stated is what not to do. We absolutely cannot afford to get into a political, cultural battle over which is the one true faith. Such conflicts only divide and escalate already palpable tensions, tearing us away from a search for what is true and refocusing us on the old petty squabbles for power, position, and cultural ascendancy. Instead, we need to make ironic resistance and its origin and permutations part of our common vernacular. In this way we can consistently remind each other of the limitations of a purely rationalist, materialist mind-set, encouraging each other to invest in a quest for faith in the unseen. This can be done through reading, research, prayers, and productive conversation within a supportive community of people dedicated to searching for truth—wherever it may be. Gradually, communities of men and women in which power agendas are subordinate to the pursuit of truth and social justice need to form and grow. In the words of theorist M.M. Bakhtin, these communities should be characterized by "diachronic discourse," in which diverse voices in pursuit of truth refine each other's metal. For the problem, as Bakhtin understood, is that we all tend to speak "monologically." We speak with limited perspective and with narrow self or group interest. The end of monologue is material power with its accompanying friends, wealth, and prestige. These, of course, are the bastard fathers of all of the false centers of meaning which have trapped men for so long. Monologue can only be broken when we come into contact with other voices different from our own. This "dialogism" causes "disharmony," a condition in which both monologic voices, so sure that they have the truth, wind up questioning themselves. Naturally, this process is at work all the time with many more voices than just two, and the hope is that within this disharmony two things will happen: Each monologic voice will gain some feelings of empathy with the other voices and each voice will be sharpened by the dialogic fire. If all parties have the pursuit of truth as their ultimate goal, we should get closer and closer to accurate understandings of how things work in our world.[242] It must be pointed out, however, that this has not happened very much in broad, group practice, though it sounds nice in theory. Why hasn't it happened? Perhaps because men have been so conditioned to pursue everything to find meaning in their lives except for truth and self-sacrifice, the very things required to give Bakhtin's ideas life. However, this is not to say that it doesn't happen in the personal lives of some men, nor do I mean to suggest that it can not happen on a wider scale. I think it can, but it will require men to take the first step of seeing through the great lie of Enlightenment rationalism, namely that meaning and purpose, the heart of masculinity, can only be found in the material realm. Only then can they begin the quest of faith along the road of Bakhtinian dialogism. Within the hearts of such people and communities perverted forms of abusive religion could be checked and healthy identities could be cultivated through identifying the self with "other;" this would not be done in an unrealistic way that does not take into account the competitive realities of life, but in a way that calls for subordination of the self to the interests of others whenever possible so as to make God's world a better place and to direct our focus toward eternal reward rather than material success. The longer we engage this process and the more men we bring into it, the healthier men will be, the healthier women and children will be, the healthier states and countries will be, the kinder the world will be, and the more, in my opinion, God will be pleased.

128

Notes

[216] Philip Roth. *American Pastoral*. (Boston: Houghton-Mifflin, 1997).

[217] Jacques Derrida. "Structure, Sign and Play in the Discourses of the Human Sciences," in Rice, Philip, ed. *Modern Literary Theory: A Reader* (New York: St. Martin's, 1996).

[218] Richard Rorty. *Contingency, Irony and Solidarity*. (Cambridge: Cambridge University Press, 1989).

[219] Carol Shields. *The Stone Diaries*. (New York: Viking, 1994) 92.

[220] Shields, 183.

[221] *Merchants of Cool*. (Boston: WGBH Educational Foundation, 2001).

[222] Don DeLillo. *White Noise*. (New York: Viking, 1985).

[223] Craig Slane. *Bonhoeffer as Martyr: Social Responsibility and Modern Christian Commitment*. (Grand Rapids, MI: Brazos, 2004).

[224] Kevin Charles Belmonte. *Hero For Humanity: A Biography of William Wilberforce*. (Colorado Springs, CO: Navpress, 2002).

[225] Barbara Kramer. *George Washington Carver: Scientist and Inventor*. (Berkeley Heights, NJ: Enslow Publishing, 2002).

[226] Donovan Fitzpatrick. *Navy Maverick: Uriah P. Levy*. (Garden City, NY: Doubleday Press, 1963).

[227] See yusafislam.org.uk.

[228] Beth Duff Brown. "Some Hindus Rescue Muslims While Others Express Shame, Regret," (Ahmadabad, India: Associated Press, March 4, 2002).

[229] Soren Kierkegaard. *Fear and Trembling*. (London: Oxford University Press, 1946) 35.

[230] Chaim Potok. *The Book of Lights*. (New York: Knopf, 1981).

[231] Cheikh Hamidou Kane. *Ambiguous Adventure*. (New York: Walker Press, 1963).

[232] Leslie Marmon Silko. *Ceremony*. (New York: Viking, 1977) 14.

[233] Silko, 222-232.

[234] Ralph Waldo Emerson. "Brahma," in Myerson, Joel, ed. *Transcendentalism: A Reader*. (Oxford: Oxford University Press, 2000) 499.

[235] Herman Hesse. *Siddhartha*. (New York: Bantam, 1971).

129

[236] Walker Percy. *Second Coming.* (New York: Pocket Books, 1981).

[237] Daniel Pipes. "The Quiet-Spoken Muslims Who Turn to Terror," (New York: The New York Sun, March 14, 2006).

[238] Mark Juergensmeyer. *Terror in the Mind of God: The Global Rise of Religious Violence.* (Berkeley, CA: University of California Press, 2001).

[239] Juergensmeyer, 109.

[240] Juergensmeyer, 168.

[241] Juergensmeyer, 171.

[242] Mikhail Bakhtin. *The Dialogic Imagination.* (Austin, TX: University of Texas Press, 2002).

131

Bibliography

Adelman, Marvin. *A Sporting Time*. Chicago: University of Illinois Press, 1986.
Aligheri, Dante. *The Divine Comedy*. New York: Oxford University Press, 1993.
Bacon, Lloyd. *Knute Rockne: All American*: Los Angeles: Warner Bros., 1940.
Bakhtin, Mikhail. *The Dialogic Imagination*. Austin, TX: University of Texas
    Press, 2002.
Barbour, Ralph Henry. *The Halfback*. New York: Grosset & Dunlap, 1899.
Beaudine, William. *Hold That Line*. Los Angeles: Warner Bros, 1952.
Belasco, David. *Six Plays by David Belasco*. Boston: Little, Brown, 1928.
Belmonte, Kevin Charles. *Hero for Humanity: A Biography of William
    Wilberforce*. Colorado Springs, CO: Navpress, 2002.
Benedek, Laszlo. *The Wild One*. Hollister, CA: Stanley Kramer Productions,
    1953.
Betts, John Rickards. *America's Sporting Heritage: 1850-1950*. Reading, MA:
    Wesley, 1974.
Bokser, Ben Zion, ed. *The Jewish Mystical Tradition*. Northvale, NJ: J. Aronson,
    1993.
Boyd, Stephen, ed. *Redeeming Men: Religion and Masculinities*. Louisville, KY:
    Westminster John Knox, 1996.
Brod, Harry, ed. *The Making of Masculinity: The New Men's Studies*. New York:
    Routledge, 1992.
Bronte, Charlotte. *Jane Eyre*. New York: Norton, 1987.
Brown, Beth Duff. "Some Hindus Rescue Muslims While Others Express Shame,
    Regret." Ahmadabad, India: *Associated Press*, March 4, 2002.
Bunyan, Paul. *The Pilgrim's Progress*. New York: Dutton, 1940.
Burns, Sarah. *Inventing the Modern Artist*. New Haven: Yale University Press,
    1996.
Campbell, Donna. *Resisting Regionalism: Gender and Naturalism in American
    Fiction: 1885-1915*. Athens, OH: Ohio University Press, 2000.
Carnes, Marc. *Secret Ritual: Manhood in Victorian America*. New Haven:
    Yale University Press, 1989.
Chesterton, G.K. *Orthodoxy*. New York: Dodd, Mead, 1950.
Chodorow, Nancy. "The Enemy Outside: Thoughts on the Psychodynamics of
    Extreme Violence with Special Attention to Men and Masculinity."

Masculinity Studies & Feminist Theories: New Directions Ed. Judith Kegan Gardiner. New York: Columbia University Press, 2002.

Chopin, Kate. *The Awakening.* New York: H.S. Stone, 1899.

Connell, Robert W. "The History of Masculinity." *The Masculinity Studies Reader* Eds. Rachel Adams and David Savran. Malden, MA: Blackwell, 2002.

Cooper, James Fenimore. *The Leatherstocking Tales.* New York: Viking, 1985.

Coover, Robert. *The Universal Baseball Association of Henry J. Waugh.* New York: New American Library, 1971.

Crane, Stephen. *The Red Badge of Courage.* New York: Modern Library, 1925.

Curtiz, Michael. *Jim Thorpe: All-American.* Los Angeles: Warner Bros., 1951.

Dagwood, N.J., ed. *Koran.* New York: Penguin, 1990.

Davis, Bill. *Dancing in the End Zone.* New York: S. French, 1985.

Davis, Rebecca Harding. *Life in Iron Mills.* Boston: Bedford Books, 1998.

Deardorff, Donald. *Sports: A Reference Guide and Critical Commentary, 1980-1999.* Westport, CT: Greenwood Press, 2001.

Defoe, Daniel. *Robinson Crusoe.* New York: Norton, 1975.

DeFord, Frank. *Everybody's All-American.* Cambridge, MA: DeCapo Press, 2004.

DeLillo, Don. *End Zone.* New York: Viking, 1972.

_____. *White Noise.* New York: Viking, 1985.

Derrida, Jacques. "Structure, Sign and Play in the Discourses of the Human Sciences." *Modern Literary Theory: A Reader* Ed. Philip Rice. New York: St. Martin's, 1996.

Deutsch, Emanuel. *The Talmud.* Philadelphia: Jewish Publication Society of America, 1896.

Dickens, Charles. *A Tale of Two Cities.* Philadelphia: Running Press, 1986.

Dreiser, Theodore. *The Financier.* New York: Harper & Brothers, 1912.

Eastwood, Clint. *Unforgiven.* Los Angeles: Warner Bros., 1992.

Ellis, Bret Easton. *American Psycho.* New York: Vintage, 1991.

Ellison, Ralph. *Invisible Man.* New York: New American Library, 1952.

Emerson, Ralph Waldo. "Brahma." *Transcendentalism: A Reader* Ed. Joel Myerson. Oxford: Oxford University Press, 2000.

Faulkner, William. *The Sound & The Fury.* New York: Modern Library, 1956.

Ferguson, Charles. *Pigskin.* New York: Doubleday, 1929.

Fitzgerald, F. Scott. *The Great Gatsby.* New York: Scribner, 1925.

Fitzpatrick, Donovan. *Navy Maverick: Uriah P. Levy.* Garden City, NY: Doubleday Press, 1963.

Ford, Richard. *Independence Day.* New York: Vintage, 1995.

Forter, Greg. *Murdering Masculinities: Fantasies of Gender and Violence in the American Crime Novel.* New York: New York University Press, 2000.

Frederick, Harold. *The Damnation of Theron Ware.* New York: Stone & Kimball, 1896.

Friedan, Betty. *The Feminine Mystique.* New York: Norton, 1963.

Friendlich, Dick. *Left End Scott.* Philadelphia: Westminster, 1955.
Gault, William. *Bruce Benedict, Halfback.* New York: Dutton, 1959.
Gent, Peter. *North Dallas Forty.* New York: Morrow, 1973.
Gibson, Mel. *Braveheart.* Los Angeles: Paramount, 1995.
Goodman, Barak. *Merchants of Cool.* Boston: WGBH Educational Foundation, 2001.
Gorn, Eliot. *The Manly Art: Bare-Knuckle Prize Fighting in America.* Ithaca, NY: Cornell University Press, 1986.
Haberstroh, Charles J. *Melville and Male Identity.* Rutherford, NJ: Fareligh Dickinson University Press, 1980.
Halberstam, David. *The Fifties.* New York: Ballantine, 1993.
Happe, Francois. "Voice and Authority in Don DeLillo's *End Zone.*" *French Review of American Studies* 54 (1992): 385.
Harkins, Philip. *Breakaway Back.* New York: W. Morrow & Co., 1959.
Hawthorne, Nathaniel. *The Scarlet Letter.* New York: New American Library, 1959.
Hemingway, Earnest. *The Sun Also Rises.* New York: Grosset & Dunlap, 1926.
Heuman, William. *Left End Luisetti.* Austin, TX: Steck & Co., 1958.
Heyliger, William. *Top Lineman.* New York: Appleton, 1943.
Herbert, T. Walter. *Sexual Violence and American Manhood.* Cambridge, MA: Harvard University Press, 2002.
Hesse, Herman. *Siddhartha.* New York: Bantam, 1971.
Hibbs, Jesse. *The All-American.* Los Angeles: Universal International Pictures, 1953.
Holden, Jonathon. "Why We Bombed Haiphong." *Real Things: An Anthology of Popular Culture in American Poetry* Eds. Jim Ellidge and Susan Swartwont. Bloomington, IN: Indiana University Press, 1999.
Holy Bible. New York: Thomas Nelson, 1952.
Howells, William Dean. *The Rise of Silas Lapham.* Boston: Houghton-Mifflin, 1888.
Hua, Hsuan. *The Sutras in Forty-Two Chapters as Divulged by the Buddha.* Howell, MI: The Buddhist Temple, 2005.
Jackson, Kenneth and David S. Dunbar, eds. *Empire City: New York Through The Ages.* New York: Columbia University Press, 2002.
James, Henry. *The Bostonians.* New York: MacMillan and Co., 1886.
Johnson, Owen. *Stover at Yale.* New York: Frederick Stokes, 1912.
Johnston, John. "Generic Difficulties in the Novels of Don DeLillo." *Critique: Studies in Modern Fiction* 30 (1989) 265.
Juergensmeyer, Mark. *Terror in the Mind of God: The Global Rise of Religious Violence.* Berkeley, CA: University of California Press, 2001.
Kane, Ccheikh Hamidou. *Ambiguous Adventure.* New York: Walker Press, 1963.
Kerouac, Jack. *On The Road.* New York: Buccanneer Books, 1957.
Kierkegaard, Soren. *Fear and Trembling.* London: Oxford University Press, 1946.

134

Kirkham, Pat and Janet Thumin, eds. *Me Jane: Masculinity, Movies and Women.* New York: St. Martin's, 1995.

Kivel, Paul. "The 'Act Like a Man' Box." *Masculinity: Interdisciplinary Readings* Ed. Mark Hussey. Upper Saddle River, NJ: Prentice-Hall, 2003.

Kramer, Barbara. *George Washington Carver: Scientist and Inventor.* Berkeley Heights, NJ: Enslow Publishing, 2002.

Kovic, Ron. *Born on the Fourth of July.* New York: McGraw-Hill, 1976.

Kucich, John. "Postmodern Politics: Don DeLillo and the Plight of the White Male Writer." *Michigan Quarterly Review* 27 (1988) 337.

Kushner, Tony. *Angels in America.* New York: Theater Communications Group, 1993.

Lampell, Millard. *The Hero.* New York: J. Messner, 1949.

LeClair, Thomas. "Deconstructing the Logos: Don DeLillo's *End Zone.*" *Modern Fiction Studies* 33 (1987): 107.

Lehman, Peter, ed. *Masculinity, Bodies, Movies, Culture.* New York: Routledge, 2001.

Levant, Ronald F. "The Masculinity Crisis." *The Men's Studies Journal* 5 (1997): 221-231.

Lewis, C.S. *Till We Have Faces.* New York: Harcourt, Brace, 1956.

London, Jack. *The Game.* New York: Collier, 1905.

Lubin, David M. *Picturing a Nation: Art and Social Change in Nineteenth Century America.* New Haven: Yale University Press, 1994.

Lyon, Francis. *Crazy Legs.* Los Angeles: Republic Pictures Productions, 1953.

McBride, James. *War, Battering and Other Sports.* Atlantic Highlands, NJ: Humanities Press, 1995.

McCormick, Wilford. *Five Yards to Glory.* New York: Grosett & Dunlap, 1959.

McElvaine, Robert. *The Great Depression: America 1929-1941.* New York: Times Books, 1984.

Melosh, Barbara, ed. *Gender and American History Since 1890.* New York: Routledge, 1993.

Melville, Herman. *Moby Dick.* New York: Vintage Books, 1991.

Messenger, Christian. *Sport and the Spirit of Play in American Fiction: Hawthorne to Faulkner.* New York: Columbia University Press, 1981.

Messner, Michael. *Power at Play.* Boston: Beacon Press, 1992.

Metalious, Grace. *Peyton Place.* New York: Dell, 1956.

Milton, John. *Paradise Lost.* New York: G. Olms, 1976.

Murphy, Ralph. *The Spirit of West Point.* Los Angeles: Bro-Rog Pictures Corp., 1947.

Naipaul, V.S. *Finding the Center.* New York: Vintage, 1986.

Narayan, R.K. *The Vendor of Sweets.* New York: Bard Books, 1967.

Ng, Franklin. *Asian Americans: Reconceptualizing Culture, History, Politics.* New York: Garland Press, 2004.

Nicholas, Ray. *Rebel Without a Cause.* Los Angeles: Warner Bros., 1955.

Norris, Frank. *Mcteague*. New York: Doubleday, 1903.

Norwood, Stephen. *Strikebreaking & Intimidation: Mercenaries & Masculinity in Twentieth-Century America*. Chapel Hill, NC: University of North Carolina Press, 2002.

Oriard, Michael. *Dreaming of Heroes: American Sports Fiction 1868-1980*. Chicago: Nelson-Hall, 1982.

_____. *Reading Football: How the Popular Press Created an American Spectacle*. Chapel Hill, NC: University of North Carolina Press, 1993.

Osteen, Mark. "Against the End: Asceticism and Apocalypse in Don Delillo's *End Zone*." *Papers on Language and Literature* 26 (1990): 148.

Percy, Walker. *Second Coming*. New York: Pocket Books, 1981.

Phurr, Suzanne. "Homophobia as a Weapon of Sexism." *Race, Class and Gender in the United States: An Integrated Study* Ed. Paula Rothenberg. New York: St. Martin's, 1992.

Pipes, Daniel. "The Quiet-Spoken Muslims Who Turn to Terror." New York: *The New York Sun*. March 14, 2006.

Potok, Chaim. *My Name is Asher Lev*. New York: Fawcett, 1972.

_____. *The Book of Lights*. New York: Knopf, 1981.

_____. *The Chosen*. New York: Fawcett, 1967.

_____. *The Promise*. New York: Fawcett, 1970.

Pugh, David. *Sons of Liberty: The Masculine Mind in Nineteenth-Century America*. Westport, CT: Greenwood Press, 1983.

Reese, Renford. *American Paradox: Young Black Men*. Durham, NC: Carolina Academic Press, 2004.

Rorty, Richard. *Contingency, Irony and Solidarity*. Cambridge: Cambridge University Press, 1989.

Rose, Kenneth. *One Nation Underground: The Fallout Shelter in American Culture*. New York: New York University Press, 2001.

Rosenberg, Warren. *Legacy of Rage: Jewish Masculinity, Violence and Culture*. Amherst, MA: University of Massachusetts Press, 2001.

Roth, Philip. *American Pastoral*. New York: Vintage, 1998.

_____. *My Life as a Man*. New York: Penguin, 1985.

Rotundo, E. Anthony. *American Manhood: Transformations from the Revolution to the Modern Era*. New York: Basic Books, 1993.

Schwalbe, Michael. *Unlocking the Iron Cage: The Men's Movement, Gender Politics, and American Culture*. New York: Oxford University Press, 1996.

Schwartz, Richard. *The 1950s*. New York: Facts on File, 2003.

Shields, Carol. *The Stone Diaries*. New York: Viking, 1994.

Silko, Leslie Marmon. *Ceremony*. New York: New American Library, 1977.

Slane, Craig. *Bonhoeffer as Martyr: Social Responsibility and Modern Christian Commitment*. Grand Rapids, MI: Brazos, 2004.

Smiley, Jane. *Good Faith*. New York: Random House, 2003.

Smith, Joseph. *The Book of Mormon*. Salt Lake City: The Church of Jesus Christ of Latter Day Saints, 1968.

Spears, Betty and Richard Swanson., eds. *History of Sport and Physical Education in the United States*. Dubuque, IA: William C. Brown Publishers, 1988.

Steinbeck, John. *The Grapes of Wrath*. New York: Viking, 1939.

Steinberg, Warren. *Masculinity: Identity, Conflict, and Transformation*. Boston: Random-House, 1993.

Stone, Oliver. *Alexander*. Los Angeles: Warner Bros., 2005.

Stowe, Harriet Beacher. *Uncle Tom's Cabin*. Boston: J.P. Jewett, 1852.

Tunis, John R. *Iron Duke*. New York: Harcourt, Brace, 1938.

Umphlett, Wiley. *The Achievement of American Sports Literature*. Toronto: Associated University Press, 1991.

Updike, John. *Rabbit Run*. New York: Knopf, 1960.

Van de Weyer. *366 Readings From Hinduism*. Cleveland, OH: The Pilgrim Press, 2000.

Veith, Gene E. *Postmodern Times: A Christian Guide to Contemporary Theory and Culture*. Wheaton, IL: Crossway Books, 1994.

Wallace, Lew. *Ben Hur*. New York: Dodd, Mead, 1953.

Walters, Charles. *Good News*. Los Angeles: MGM, 1947.

Wesley, Marilyn. *Violent Adventure: Contemporary Fiction of American Men*. Charlottesville, VA: University of Virginia Press, 2003.

West, Russell. *Subverting Masculinity: Hegemonic and Alternative Versions of Masculinity in Contemporary Culture*. Atlanta: Rodopi Press, 2001.

White, Kevin. *The First Sexual Revolution: The Emergence of Male Heterosexuality in America*. New York: New York University Press, 1993.

Whitehead, James. *Joiner*. New York: Knopf, 1971.

Wilder, Laura Ingalls. *Little House on the Prairie*. New York: Harper, 1953.

Wilson, Sloan. *Man in the Gray Flannel Suit*. New York: Simon & Schuster, 1955.

Wolfe, Tom. *The Bonfire of the Vanities*. New York: Farrar, Straus, Giroux, 1989.

Zophy, Angela Howard. *Handbook of Women's History*. New York: Garland Reference Library, 1990.

Index

48, 49, 51, 130, 132, 133   Zohar, 115, 116